W9-BZH-853

REDWOOD

LIBRARY
NEWPORT
R.I.

GARDNER BLANCHARD PERRY FUND

WITHDRAWN

O Canada

BOOKS BY EDMUND WILSON

I THOUGHT OF DAISY

AXEL'S CASTLE

THE TRIPLE THINKERS

TO THE FINLAND STATION

THE WOUND AND THE BOW

THE SHOCK OF RECOGNITION

MEMOIRS OF HECATE COUNTY

EUROPE WITHOUT BAEDEKER

CLASSICS AND COMMERCIALS

THE SHORES OF LIGHT

FIVE PLAYS

THE SCROLLS FROM THE DEAD SEA

RED, BLACK, BLOND AND OLIVE

A PIECE OF MY MIND

THE AMERICAN EARTHQUAKE

APOLOGIES TO THE IROQUOIS

WILSON'S NIGHT THOUGHTS

PATRIOTIC GORE

THE COLD WAR AND THE INCOME TAX

O CANADA

O Canada

AN AMERICAN'S
NOTES ON
CANADIAN CULTURE

by

EDMUND WILSON

FARRAR, STRAUS AND GIROUX • NEW YORK

Copyright © 1964, 1965 by Edmund Wilson
Library of Congress catalog card number 65-13730
All rights reserved
First printing, 1965
Nearly all of the material in this book originally appeared
in the *New Yorker* in a somewhat different form

Published simultaneously in Canada by
Ambassador Books, Ltd., Toronto
Manufactured in the United States of America

148896

W692

PR
9153
.W5
1965

O Canada

MAY 1 4 '65

My introduction to the cultural life of Canada took place nine summers ago when, after attending the Stratford Festival, I visited Toronto for the first time and, through the kindness of Mr. Robert Weaver, an official of CBS who supervises its cultural programs and the editor of the magazine called the *Tamarack Review*, was enabled to meet some of the people in the literary and academic worlds. At that time, I read Morley Callaghan's novel *The Loved and the Lost* and, later, *The Many Colored Coat*, and I wrote an article about them. I am letting this article stand here, with a supplement in which I deal with his other novels, somewhat apart from my notes on Canadian culture, written at a later date, which treat mainly of Canadian writers in relation to their own country, as Mr. Callaghan's fiction stands somewhat apart from local preoccupations. I have since this article was written paid several visits to Canada and have seen something both there and abroad of Canadians interested in literature. Among these, I must acknowledge debts for advice, information and materials, besides that to Mr. Weaver,

3

to Mr. Pierre Berton, Mr. Callaghan and his family, and Mr. Malcolm Montgomery of Toronto; to Mr. John Buell, Mr. Louis Dudek, Mr. Hugh MacLennan and Mr. Leslie Roberts of Montreal; to Mlle Marie-Claire Blais, M. Jean-Charles Falardeau, Mlle Jeanne Lapointe and M. Roger Lemelin of Quebec; and to Miss Marine Leland of Smith College. While working on these notes during a winter in Paris, I was fortunate in being able to see something of M. Gilles Couture and Mrs. Mavis Gallant, who afforded me invaluable assistance in getting me books from the French Canadian Library and in helping to fill in for me the Canadian background. And I owe a special kind of debt to Mr. Peter Gzowski and the other editors of *Maclean's Magazine*, as well as to M. Paul-Marie Lapointe, the editor of the French edition, both for their helpfulness in telling me what I wanted to know and for the articles in their magazines, upon which I have often drawn. Mr. Gzowski and his associates succeeded in transforming *Maclean's* from a rather inferior version of the kind of thing that we get in *McCall's* or the *Saturday Evening Post* into an outstanding journalistic achievement, an enterprising and intelligent coverage—the fiction department having been dropped —of all phases of Canadian life, by what I suppose must have been one of the ablest staffs ever got together in Canada. It is regrettable that a change of management which involved putting a curb on the free expression of the findings and views of these writers should have resulted in the resignation of almost the whole staff and converted the magazine back again

4

from a serious venture in reporting to an exploit in the higher pulp. I am indebted to Mr. F. R. Scott for permission to reprint his satirical poem; to Miss Mary Meigs for permission to reproduce her portrait of Mlle Blais; and to Mr. Duncan Macpherson for permission to reproduce his cartoons.

Though I have made no attempt in what follows to do justice to everybody and everything, I do feel a certain compunction at having skimped the Scottish end of Canadian culture, and I want to recommend here the recent book about his Scottish Canadian origins by Mr. John Kenneth Galbraith, called *The Scotch* in America and *Made to Last* in England. It is a very good thing that Mr. Galbraith did not try to make a regional novel out of the harsh rather gloomy life of his locality in south-western Ontario. That novel would have been a bore as so many such novels are. But the little book he has written—quite free from Scottish sentimentality—gives a hard realistic picture of the strengths and the limitations of Scottish Canadian character. To this I would add the descriptions, amusing and acutely observed, of middle-class Scottish Canadian households, in Mavis Gallant's new book of short stories, *My Heart is Broken*. Mrs. Gallant, though not Catholic or French in origin, was educated in a French Quebec convent and knows French as well as Scottish Canada. She is more international than Canadian and in these later more elaborate stories, as in her novel *Green Water, Green Sky*, adventuring about Europe, she gets away from the Canadian bleakness and her work displays a color and wit rather rare

5

among native writers. She is excellent at evoking, by dialogue and detail, a variety of milieux, and the stories about Canada gain from their contrast with those that take place in the other parts of the world she has inhabited. But she has not quite found her form and her stance. These stories are likely to impress one as being not so much real short stories as episodes from some larger fiction—the projection of a mixed experience—that she has not yet found out how to manage, and even the episodes of her novel itself give something of this impression. Mrs. Gallant now lives mostly in France, and one feels that there may here be involved a difficulty of national identity which makes her orientations uncertain. Younger than Hugh MacLennan, she is, like him, a brilliant example of the Canadian cosmopolitan; but whereas Mr. MacLennan now writes almost exclusively about Canadian society, Mrs. Gallant feels no dedication to it. This liberty of movement, however, gives a certain artistic freedom which, in spite of the uncomfortable character of many of Mrs. Gallant's subjects and the sleaziness of many of her types, brings a certain exhilaration.

Morley Callaghan of Toronto

THE Canadian Morley Callaghan, at one time well known in the United States, is today perhaps the most unjustly neglected novelist in the English-speaking world. In his youth, he worked on the Toronto *Star* —Toronto is his native city—at the time when Ernest Hemingway had a job on the same paper, and, through Hemingway, who took his manuscripts to Paris, some of Callaghan's early short stories were accepted by Ezra Pound for his little magazine *Exile*. Maxwell Perkins of Scribner's was impressed by these stories and had them reprinted in *Scribner's Magazine*, which later published other stories by Callaghan. His novels were published by Scribner's. Morley Callaghan was a friend of Fitzgerald and Hemingway and was praised by Ring Lardner, and he belonged to the literary scene of the twenties. He appeared in *transition* as well as in *Scribner's* and he spent a good deal of his time in Paris and the United States. But eventually he went back to Canada, and it is one of the most striking signs of the partial isolation of that country from the rest of the cultural world that—in spite of the fact that

9

his stories continued to appear in The *New Yorker* up to the end of the thirties—he should quickly have been forgotten in the United States and should be almost unknown in England. Several summers ago, on a visit to Toronto, I had given me a copy of the Canadian edition of a novel of his called *The Loved and the Lost*. It seemed to me so remarkable that I expected it to attract attention in England and the United States. But it was never published in England, and it received so little notice in the United States that I imagined it had not been published here either. I found that when I talked about Callaghan, such people as remembered his existence were likely to think he was dead. When I checked; I discovered that the book *had* been published here without ever having been adequately reviewed, but that it had later sold well in paperback. A volume of Morley Callaghan's collected short stories was published last year in Toronto but not in the United States or England. This season a new novel by him—*The Many Colored Coat*—has been brought out simultaneously in Canada and in New York.

I want to talk in this review about both these two novels of Callaghan's—I have read only one of his earlier books—and to speculate first on the reasons for the current indifference to his work. This has no doubt been partly due to the peculiar relation of Canada to England and the United States. The Canadian background of Morley Callaghan's stories seems alien to both these other countries and at the same time not strange enough to exercise the spell of the truly exotic. To the reviewer, this background has much interest and charm. Montreal, with its snow-dazzling mountain, its passionate winter sports, its hearty and busy bars, its jealously guarded French culture, and its pealing of bells from French churches, side by side with the solid Presbyterianism of its Anglo-Scottish best people, is a world I find it pleasant to explore. It is curious to see how much this world has been influenced—in its language, in its amusements, its press—by the "Americans," as they still call us, and how far —in, for example, its parliamentary politics and its social and moral codes—it rests on somewhat different foundations. But Mr. Callaghan is not writing about Canada at all from the point of view of exploiting its regional characteristics. In the second of these two novels, he does not even tell the reader that the scene of the story is Montreal. The landscapes, the streets and the houses, the atmosphere of the various milieux are known intimately and sensitively observed, but they are made to figure quite unobtrusively; there are no very long descriptions and nothing like "documentation." We simply find ourselves living with the characters and taking for granted, as they do, their habits and customs and assumptions, their near-Arctic climate and their split nationality. Still less is Mr. Callaghan occupied with specifically Canadian problems. The new and militant Canadian nationalism—in these novels, at least—does not touch him; he is not here concerned with the question of "what it means to be a Canadian." And the result of this has been, I believe, that a public, both here and in England, whose taste in American fiction seems to have been largely whetted

11

by the perpetrators of violent scenes—and these include some of our best writers as well as our worst—does not find itself at home with, does not really comprehend, the more sober effects of Callaghan. In his novels one finds acts of violence and a certain amount of sensuality, but these are not used for melodrama or even for "symbolic" fables of the kind that is at present fashionable. There are no love stories that follow an expected course, not even any among those I have read that eventually come out all right. It is impossible to imagine these books transposed into any kind of terms that would make them acceptable to Hollywood.

The novels of Morley Callaghan do not deal, then, with his native Canada in any editorial or informative way, nor are they aimed at any popular taste, Canadian, "American" or British. They center on situations of primarily psychological interest that are treated from a moral point of view yet without making moral judgments of any conventional kind, and it is in consequence peculiarly difficult to convey the implications of one of these books by attempting to retell its story. The revelation of personality, of tacit conflict, of reciprocal emotion is conducted in so subtle a way that we are never quite certain what the characters are up to—they are often not certain themselves—or what the upshot of their relationships will be.

In the earlier of the two novels under discussion, *The Loved and the Lost* (not, perhaps, a very happy title), an eccentric but attractive young girl who exerts a mysterious spiritual charm, the daughter of a minister who has lost his faith, has become—as the

Morley Callaghan. *Photograph by Barry Callaghan*

result of a girlhood association, particularly warm and close, with the one colored family in her neighborhood—much addicted to the society of Negroes. After graduating from college in Montreal, she continues to live in that city, and goes often to a Negro night club, at which she becomes so well known to the customers and the management both that they regard her as a part of the establishment. This arouses the suspicions of her white employers and eventually makes her Negro friends uncomfortable. The former assume that she has Negro lovers and decide not to keep her on, and the latter do not know what to make of her. She evidently—though we are never told explicitly—does not sleep with either her white or her colored admirers, but she inevitably, though unintentionally, causes trouble in this little Negro world by exciting, through the fascination she exercises, the jealousies of the whites against the Negroes and of the Negroes among themselves. In the meantime, she is kind and generous to Negroes and whites alike, except when someone tries to deflect her from what is bound to appear to her non-colored friends an unsuitable mode of life, and both feel that they get from her something which is not of the conventional world and which either, with finer natures, inspires a devoted if disquieted respect or, with grosser ones, spurs them to "possess" her and thus to get the better of something that challenges and teases and balks them without their understanding why. Having lost all her office jobs—to the scandal of her educated acquaintances—she is reduced to working in a factory, which, however, she seems not in the least to mind. She is actually a kind of saint, and yet nothing is more admirable in the novel than the way in which Mr. Callaghan never lapses into mysticism or sentimentality but always makes her a believable girl. Her way of talking, her way of dressing, her involuntary reactions to people are always of the human world, and she has moments, when lectured or importuned, of something approaching bitchiness. The reasons for her puzzling behavior are in one sense sufficiently accounted for by her first having experienced, in girlhood, a feeling of sexual ecstasy at the sight of a nude Negro boy. But this feeling had come to her, she says, as a sudden and sharp realization that "beauty could be painful in a strange way," and one assumes that there has always been a barrier—from a kind of noble purity, apparently, as much as if not more than from racial inhibition—that has kept her from any more intimate contact. She is one of those virginal women, independent and idealistic, who elicit a wondering awe yet who pique the ego of others. The whole story is told from the point of view of a young university professor, Jim McAlpine, who has not wanted to fall in love with her but who finds that he cannot keep away from her and has been trying to make her extricate herself from the dangerous anomalies of her life yet who cannot quite understand her and is himself never able to rid himself of the suspicions of deceit and depravity that she inspires in her other acquaintances. The point is that none of these people can rise to the level of believing that such a person as she exists. In the end, a nasty brawl in the night club is provoked by her presence there, and she is raped and strangled that night by a white man who has been laying siege to her, who has set off the brawl in the night club by his brutal advances in public and who has been badly beaten up by the Negroes.

In the other of these novels, *The Many Colored Coat*, a young man named Harry Lane, personable, able and popular, and on the edge of Montreal's upper crust, has proved a spectacular success in a public-relations job for a Canadian whisky distiller. He forms a friendship that to some seems incongruous with an amiable but very middle-class bank manager whose quietness and modesty and apparent good sense the young man finds reassuring in contrast to the company of those whom he is constantly, in the line of business, gladhanding and entertaining. But this middle-aged man, who seems sound and wise, is to become in his turn so beglamored by the handsome and delightful Harry that he cannot help desiring for himself a little more of the freedom of Harry's world and for his son some of Harry's advantages. An old friend of Harry's turns up, who, out of gratitude for former kindness, has made him a present of some "Western Oil" stock. Now that a drilling is about to take place, the shares will be immensely valuable, and he will sell him some more at a dollar apiece. The manager offers Harry a loan from the bank and succeeds in putting it through, but only by misrepresenting—though Harry does not know this—the amount of his friend's security, which consists of the shares he already owns; then, rather to Harry's surprise, he asks for a slice of the stock in

15

return for negotiating the loan. He hopes, of course, to make good the difference between the fraudulent figure and the real one from the profits to accrue from the stock. But "Western Oil" now turns out to be worthless, and the manager is sent to jail. He kills himself in prison without having let it be known that it was he who proposed the loan and that he wanted some of the stock for himself, leaving Harry to bear the odium of having ruined the much-respected banker by inducing him to commit a fraud. Not to be liked is for Harry intolerable; it completely throws him off his base and makes him unexpectedly vindictive. But this does not help the situation. He suffers the fate of Joseph, who has been envied by his brethren for his many-colored coat—that is, for his popularity, his easy superiority. His old companions put him in Coventry, and in his vehemence to assert his innocence, to avenge himself on the dead man who has wronged him, he is carried to grotesque and almost lunatic lengths. He becomes such an obnoxious character that he can no longer have any value as a public-relations man, and his boss has to let him go. He has started a feud with a tailor, an ex-pugilist friend of the bank manager's who has always distrusted Harry and who, at the trial, has given testimony against him which, though based on a conversation misunderstood, has convinced the jury of Harry's guilt. They finally come to blows in a restaurant, and it is only when Harry, badly injured, is beginning to clear up in a hospital that he knows he has behaved ignobly. The author seems to leave him at the moment just before he is to wake to the horror

16

of realizing that he himself, through the falsity and fatuity of his previous life, has actually shared in the guilt of his friend and let him in for his sordid disaster. The ex-pugilist, brought again into court to answer for his assault on Harry, now confesses quite gratuitously and to the horror of his lawyer that he had never really known what had happened between Harry and his friend the bank manager and that he had never had the right to judge Harry.

The danger in retelling the story of this remarkable novel is that the subject may sound so unpromising that one cannot succeed in suggesting the interest which Mr. Callaghan has made it generate. These stories are extremely well told. The details, neither stereotyped nor clever—the casual gestures of the characters, the little incidents that have no direct bearing on their purposes or their actions, the people they see in restaurants or pass on the street—have a naturalness that gives the illusion of not having been invented, of that seeming irrelevance of life that is still somehow inextricably relevant. The narrative moves quietly but rapidly, and Mr. Callaghan is a master of suspense. The first hundred pages of *The Many Colored Coat* are an excellent example of this. Nothing overtly exciting occurs; the characters—though with quietly changing relationships—seem to be following the routines of normal lives, yet you know you are approaching a climax without ever having been given a hint of what this climax is going to be. The style is very clear and spare, sometimes a bit commonplace, but always intent on its purpose, always making exactly its points so that these novels are as different as possible from the contemporary bagful of words that forms the substance of so many current American books which are nevertheless taken seriously. (The one conspicuous lapse from this standard in *The Many Colored Coat* is page 208, on which "husky" or "huskily" occurs three times, having previously occurred just before, on page 205, in the same general context, and on which you find the following somewhat cockeyed sentence: "This time she was like herself as they had known her in her good days and those deep warm erotic notes came out huskily and exultant, one shoulder strap falling off, and she went on singing, her face aglow with pride and happiness, letting them see she could have sung all night." It may happen with even a very careful writer who scrupulously rewrites and revises that there is always some page or passage which he slights—whether because it deals with something that bores him or because he knows it isn't right but doesn't know how to correct it or because of some personal anxiety which afflicted him at the time of writing and of which he shrinks from being reminded.) Mr. Callaghan's underplaying of drama and the unemphatic tone of his style are accompanied by a certain grayness of atmosphere, but this might also be said of Chekhov, whose short stories his sometimes resemble.

These books, so unconventional in subject, are at the same time expertly "plotted." The motivations are handled with such delicacy that one hesitates to say there are moments when this plotting seems a little contrived. Both the novels involve young men as to

18

whom it is assumed at the beginning that they are going to marry young girls—more or less sympathetic and intelligent—of the Anglicizing upper class. In each case, this central young man is to become completely demoralized and irremediably alienated from his fiancée by something that comes from outside that class and eventually excludes him from it. McAlpine in *The Loved and the Lost* falls in love with the offbeat girl; Harry Lane in *The Many Colored Coat* is derailed by his friendship with the bank manager. Both are left adrift, almost friendless, wandering about in the streets, alone with their guilty misgivings, which it will take them a long time to allay. But the reader is troubled a little, in connection with certain turns of the narrative, by the feeling that the author has given a push to land these unreliable young men in their miserable situations. One finds it rather hard to believe that McAlpine would have left his frightened girl alone and unprotected in her room. After the ugly affair in the night club, he had, to be sure, very honorable reasons reasons for not wanting, under the circumstances, to make love to the girl that night, when she was willing for the first time, apparently, to surrender herself to him, but he had previously seen somebody prowling about and it was obvious that she needed to be reassured. Should he not have been aware of the danger and spent the night in her room? In the case of the downfall of Harry Lane, it hardly seems probable that his fellow-townsmen—almost, it seems, to a man—should have been ready to believe the worst of him.

But one's tendency, in writing of these novels, to

19

speak of what the characters "should have" done is a proof of the extraordinary effect of reality which—by simply presenting their behavior—Mr. Callaghan succeeds in producing. His people, though the dramas they enact have more than individual significance, are never allowed to appear as anything other than individuals. They never become types or abstractions, nor do they ever loom larger than life. They are never removed from our common humanity, and there is never any simple opposition of beautiful and horrible, of lofty and base. The tragedies in these two books are the results of the interactions of the weaknesses and strengths of several characters, none of whom is either entirely responsible or entirely without responsibility for the outcome that concerns them all. But in order to describe these books properly, one must explain that the central element in them, the spirit that pervades the whole, is deeply if undogmatically Christian. Though they depend on no scaffolding of theology, though they embody an original vision, they have evidently somewhere behind them the tradition of the Catholic Church. This is not the acquired doctrine of the self-conscious Catholic convert—of Graham Greene or Evelyn Waugh. One is scarcely aware of doctrine; what one finds is, rather, an intuitive sense of the meaning of Christianity. An earlier novel, *Such Is My Beloved*, which was first published in 1934 and has now been reprinted in paperback, deals with a Catholic priest who both undercuts and transcends the official level of his Church—in his unworldliness, he has something in common with the girl of *The Loved and the Lost*—and who, making a certain genuine if precarious connection with the sinners he wishes to befriend but becoming an embarrassment to his bishop, is reprimanded by this superior and alienated from the objects of his solicitude: two prostitutes, who are forced to leave town. Thus cruelly driven in on himself, he loses all contact with reality, or what the world considers reality, and is sent to a mental institution, where, in his madness, he seems to touch sanctity. So the keynote of *The Many Colored Coat* is sounded by a Catholic priest—in the only scene in which he appears—who attempts, without any success, to convey to the indignant Harry Lane that his behavior is dictated by spiritual pride. But in these two most recent novels of Callaghan's, this sense of Christian moral values is introduced even more unobtrusively than the Canadian climate and landscape and the true motivations of the characters.

The reviewer, at the end of this article, after trying to give an account of these books, is now wondering whether the primary reason for the current under-estimation of Morley Callaghan may not be simply a general incapacity—apparently shared by his compatriots—for believing that a writer whose work may be mentioned without absurdity in association with Chekhov's and Turgenev's can possibly be functioning in Toronto.

November 26, 1960

1964. Since writing the above article, I have read the rest of Callaghan's early novels, and I find that the theme of unacknowledged guilt, which figures in *The Many Colored Coat*, is central to several of them. It already appears in *Strange Fugitive* (1928), the first of his full-length fictions. This original and very curious, though unsatisfactory, book—said to be the first of the gangster novels—is the story of Harry Trotter, an almost amoeba-like creature, who, losing his job in a lumber yard and unable to find another which will give him the authority he craves, drifts along for a time, doing nothing, as he dreams of a position of power. His only way of satisfying this thirst is by an obsessional compulsion to play checkers, at which he knows he can beat his wife and friends. At one time he haunts labor meetings and sees himself as a leader but the cause of labor does not touch him. He aimlessly abandons his wife, who feels a need, unintelligible to him, of supplementing her meager life by recourse to the Catholic Church, and takes up with a woman who asks nothing of him because she sleeps with everyone else as well. Then, one evening, when walking with a friend, he sees a bootleg truck being unloaded and is seized by an impulse to hijack it. He succeeds, and he and the friend go into the bootleg business and engage in gangster wars with their rivals. Harry is quite unscrupulous and seems indifferent to the cruelty of his crimes. After murdering one of these rivals, he makes a point of attending the funeral and expressing his sympathy to the widow. But he then makes a pilgrimage to his mother's grave and has a huge and costly stone erected on it. Then he gives a gigantic dinner, which is the great high point of his life, at which everybody dances and gets drunk and which gives him immense satisfaction, for he feels that he is now a big shot. Yet he knows that he is suspected by the murdered man's friends and, after an ominous interview with them, moved apparently by a yearning for affection, he calls up his deserted wife. But he is never to see her again, for, going out with two of his pals, they are mowed down by sawed-off shot-guns. *Strange Fugitive* fails to convince because, in spite of Harry's turning to his wife and mother, he is never made sufficiently attaching, he is given no moral life. In spite of his monument to his mother, he is never actually shown either as suffering from qualms of conscience or as attempting to justify himself. The external world in which Harry moves is accurately described in detail, but he seems to be walking through it in his sleep. What the author is trying to do is present one of the lower forms of human life as, in the words of Professor F. W. Watt of Toronto University, "a kind of automaton, unable to express himself, scarcely conscious of the passions and social forces that mold and impel him." But we feel that it is impossible for Morley Callaghan really to imagine such a man. He cannot put himself in Harry's skin.

It is therefore a little surprising to find Mr. Callaghan returning to this theme—in his fourth novel, *They Shall Inherit the Earth* (1935)—in terms of a more complex and civilized world. Michael Aikenhead, a young civil engineer, who resents his father's second marriage, motivated by hateful jealousy, allows his stepbrother to drown and when his father comes under suspicion of having made away with the boy, who has been a great nuisance to everybody, he does nothing to correct this rumor, which is spoiling the reputation of the advertizing agency for which the elder Aikenhead works and which eventually costs the latter his job. The preversity and callousness of Michael's behavior, as he goes on with his own career, his unwillingness not merely to exonerate his father but to admit to himself what he is doing, is perhaps, in such a relatively civilized man as Michael is supposed to be, even more unconvincing than Harry Trotter's insensibility to his crimes and cannot but undermine the reader's interest in an otherwise rather interesting book, which deals with Canadian life in a somewhat more various way than the author's previous novels. In between these two novels, however, the author had written another—*It's Never Over* (1930)—in which the same theme, though, perhaps, even here the story seems a little forced, is exploited in a more telling way. John Hughes, out of moral cowardice, drops a girl who is very much in love with him and whom in the normal course of things he would undoubtedly have married, because her brother, a friend of his, has been found guilty of murder and hanged. This hot-tempered friend, after serving in the war, had killed a policeman who slugged him in a speakeasy raid by crashing a chair over his head. Hughes now has an affair with a girl who has been in love with the friend and is obliged at the same time to look on at the ostracism and desperate decline of the sister. His continued association with the sister of a man who has been hanged is to lead on one occasion to her coming to see him in his lodgings, and this, when the story gets around, to the scandal of Toronto respectability, results in his being dismissed from the job in a church choir on which his livelihood has mainly depended. The fatal invisible weakness which, in so many of Callaghan's novels, is made to flaw the central character, which in this case has made John Hughes fail in loyalty, gives rise to worse and worse situations, and in the course of this he becomes demoralized to a degree which reduces him to a level far below that of the more primitive friend who had unintentionally killed a policeman. The fate of the girl he has so badly treated becomes for him a constant reproach, an accusation he cannot face; and his suppressed bad conscience is made more acute, in one of the book's best scenes, by a talk with the priest, half-drunk, who had had to officiate at the hanging and who is still deeply troubled by this. John Hughes now becomes obsessed with the delusion that it is the girl who is destroying *him*, and in his mania he is driven to decide that his only course now is to kill her. He is only prevented from doing so by the discovery that she is dying of pneumonia—which, however, leaves him little less guilty, since he himself, by his behavior toward her, has been the primary agent of her moral collapse. In *Strange Fugitive*, the local descriptions appear to be disproportionate and extraneous to the human situation. But here the rather grim environment of a Toronto intimately lived—the frozen streets, the

25

moonlight on garage roofs, the snow slanting in from the black lake, the cathedral with its lighted cross, the brown hedge and the cinder path of the cemetery above the ravine—are not allowed to become monotomous but are made most effectively to merge with the uncomfortable personal relations, the insoluble emotional problems, the stifled guilt that at last takes possession in the dark lie of an insane fixation.

This condensation of a local atmosphere is very much less in evidence in Morley Callaghan's later books, where the locality is taken for granted and only very lightly sketched in. But it is a feature of *The Varsity Story* of 1948. This story is unique among Callaghan's books. It is the only one of his works in which the main subject is a local institution: the University of Toronto. One imagines that it was written in response to some suggestion on the part of the University itself, of which Mr. Callaghan is a graduate. It seems clear that he had wished, affectionately, at the same time to criticize and to celebrate. In order to accomplish this, he invents for his real university an imaginary president from New Zealand, who is at first rather contemptuous of Toronto: "Pictures like this one [a landscape painting] had built up his expectations of the country. He had dreamed of brooding northern landscapes. That first summer-time he had gone on a fishing trip to the north shore of Lake Superior and there in the blue Algoma hills had looked upon this sombre operatic country and felt its remote loneliness, and had seen the great hills rising like cathedrals against the slashes of light made by the setting sun. In the loneliness he had found grandeur. The whole countryside, the northland, the prairies, the deep rivers, accentuated in his mind his belief that in such a land and among its people there would be a poetry, a wildness or a harsh strength. He had seemed to hear the music of Sibelius. Even the extremes of climate, the unbearably hot summers and the fiercely cold winters, suggested an extreme of character in the people, a vigour, a passion. But in this city and at this university he had felt only a dismal lack of passion. Even among the students who should be so alive and so open to intellectual stimulation, and among the Faculty men, too, he had found a peculiar mildness and a lack of true affability and charm. As a city Toronto had a reticent coldness. In other Ontario towns and in the West they jeered at Toronto. But he had soon learned that many of these places were simply smaller Torontos. The more bitterly they mocked at Toronto the more conscious they seemed to be that the Toronto spirit was a skeleton hidden in their own closets."

But as the New Zealander gets to know the place better, he comes to find it more interesting and sympathetic; yet is puzzled at not being able to discover what kind of ideals the University represents, what general purpose it proposes to serve. The point is that the University of Toronto differs from our universities in the United States in being composed of a number of colleges which are dominated by different faiths and different points of view. There is a Catholic college, St. Michael's; an Anglican college, Trinity; an Evangelical college, Victoria; a non-denominational humanities college, University; and a School of Practical Science. The new president finds this confusing and cannot pin the professors down to any clear definition of what they are trying to do; but he finally comes to the conclusion that this cluster of colleges, which are dedicated to often mutually exclusive ideas, are the facets of "a giant crystal," each of which is "an aspect of the truth," which together, for the poet or philosopher, may contribute to some larger comprehension of life. This crystal is made to take shape among the gray skies and stones of Toronto, among its fogs, snows and drizzling rains, through which the facets glint and which are invested, not as in *It's Never Over* with the malaise of a coming horror, but with the dignity of human strivings. It is rather impressive evidence of Morley Callaghan's power as an artist that, in a book undertaken, apparently, for a definite practical purpose, he is able to perform this feat.

My further reading of Callaghan's novels has suggested another reason from the one proposed in my article for their relative unpopularity. Almost all of them end in annihilating violence or, more often, in blank unfulfilment. The bootlegger of *Strange Fugitive* is left riddled and dying in the street; the ex-convict of *More Joy in Heaven*, who has been doing his best to go straight but has found himself unable to free himself from his old underworld connections, shoots a policeman and is shot by the police. John Hughes of *It's Never Over*, who has shabbily abandoned one girl, becomes eventually odious to the other

28

and is dismissed by her without much sympathy: "It was such a cold wind it was more important Lillian should not miss the car than that they should go on talking." John still has his serviceable voice but he does not know how to use it: he only knows that he must go somewhere else; and Sam Raymond, in *A Passion in Rome* (1961), who, discarded by the nightclub singer whom he has rescued from alcoholism and established as a star attraction, can only hope to make up for the failure of his early aspirations as a painter by also going somewhere else and becoming a top photographer—an ambition in which the reader has no confidence that he will succeed. Marion Gibbons, in *A Broken Journey*, who is supposed to be highly sexed, feels constrained to renounce her two lovers, and leaves one of them lying half-paralyzed among the wilds of a northern lake. He has, to be sure, a sympathetic brother who will look after him, perhaps get him back to civilization, but one is not left with any suggestion as to what will become of either of them. The young professor of *The Loved and the Lost*, who had failed to stay with Peggy Sanders on the night when she was raped and strangled, is seen in the last pages desolately tramping the streets as he looks for a little church, from which he hopes for some consolation but which he is not able to find; the ex-publicity man of *The Many Colored Coat* is also left roaming the streets with no discernible future. In fact, the little drawing on the title page of *The Loved and the Lost* of a man in an overcoat, with his head bowed and his shoulders hunched, walking past a café in a snowstorm, might serve as a frontispiece

29

for a number of Callaghan's novels. Even President Tyndall of *The Varsity Story*, after a public affirmation of faith in the value of the University, on the eve of his departure for the war, is—it seems to one, quite unnecessarily—made to fall a victim to the Toronto winter and be prostrated with an influenza which the doctor fears may turn to pneumonia and from which the reader is sure that this good man will not recover. The only positive ending in these novels is that of *They Shall Inherit the Earth*, in which the sinner expiates his sin, under the influence of his lower-class Ukrainian wife, one of the meek who shall inherit the earth, by confessing it to his father and restoring their broken relations. As for the saints or near-saints of these novels, the too-innocent priest of *Such Is My Beloved* is consigned to an insane asylum, and the Negro-haunting heroine of *The Loved and the Lost* is headed for her own destruction. All these endings have their moral point: recognition of personal guilt, loyalty in personal relationships, the nobility of some reckless devotion to a Christian ideal of love which is bound to come to grief in the world. But they are probably too bleak for the ordinary reader, who may already have been disconcerted by beginning what seems to be an ordinary novel—a love story that does not go quite smoothly but which one does not expect to be wrecked or the story of a sympathetic sinner who in the end ought to be redeemed—and then finding that there is something not just temporarily but fundamentally and permanently wrong and that matters are getting out of hand, with no hope of escaping disaster. But only a

30

very sober, self-disciplined and "self-directed" writer could have persisted, from decade to decade, in submitting these parables to the public. They are almost invariably tragic, but their tragedy avoids convulsions and it allows itself no outbreak in tirades.

1

PRELUDE. The relation of Canada to the United States has always been rather peculiar. The constant slight strain it involves is to be felt in the inveterate Canadian habit, always surprising to us, of referring to us as "the Americans," as if Canadians were not Americans, too. The reason for this is apparently that at the time of our 1776 revolution "the Americans" were seditious malcontents who rebelled against their status of British colonists and set up an anti-British republic. "The Americans," for a Tory like Samuel Johnson, were always to be referred to contemptuously because they had made trouble for the monarchy. The Canadians remained British, so were never in this sense Americans, and we were for long and are sometimes still disapprovingly regarded as a society founded on disloyalty to the sovereign and the destruction of ancient traditions, and devoted to the exploits of a vulgar success which are impious in both their mutinous origins and their insolence in surpassing the mother country.

To this attitude on the part of the Canadians, the

35

Americans—if we must accept their name for us—have never paid much attention. In my youth, of the early nineteen-hundreds, we tended to imagine Canada as a kind of vast hunting preserve convenient to the United States. There is a tradition in North America—it resembles the myth of Antæus, who, in order to regain his strength, was obliged to renew his contact with the earth—that it is necessary from time to time to revindicate one's right to the continent by reverting to the life of the pioneer, by pressing on farther and farther, by exploring unvisited wilds, by inviting the challenge of hardship. In the West, at the end of the century, one still had a large choice of challenges—the forested mountains of New Mexico, the barren hills of Nevada, unexpected natural wonders and alien aborigines who were sometimes hostile, sometimes friendly—and even in the Middle West the Great Lakes and northern Michigan could satisfy this appetite for roughing it. But we Easterners were much more likely to send out our "long long thoughts" toward Canada. There the men of my father's generation hunted big game and fished for trout and salmon. It was their pride to come back with trophies in the shape of mounted moose or stag heads or unusually large fish stuffed and glazed and exhibited on oval slabs. They liked to think they had been losing themselves, escaping from the trials and anxieties of a precarious commercial society, which was always uncomfortably oscillating between booms in which people made fortunes and crashes which might leave them stripped—a society in which genteel convention now ran contrary to the poker and whis-

36

key which had been necessary to sustain their fore-
bears. They sometimes maintained permanent camps
in which they reverted to these pastimes, and had
season after season the same half-breed guide, whose
sayings they delighted to tell about at the family dinner table. In my youth, I always thought of Canada
as an inconceivably limitless extension of the wilderness—the "North Woods"—of upstate New York,
where the family spent every summer not far from
Sackets Harbor, celebrated for one of our victories
when, in the War of 1812, we were fighting the Canadian Loyalists, and not very many miles from Cape
Vincent, the old seigneurial French port where the St.
Lawrence flows out of Lake Ontario. Canada comes
back to me from childhood as a realm of huge forests,
frozen lakes, large and dangerous animals—animals
which, however, in Ernest Seton Thompson's stories,
seemed to constitute a special race that was capable of
communicating with men, of becoming our fierce foes
or our loyal allies; of Algernon Blackwood's Wendigo
(derived from the Indian legend of a cannibalistic horror), who left enormous prints in the snow and who
led the curious traveller into otherwise untrodden voids
of solitude from which he never returned; of the dashing hunters and Indians of Frederic Remington's pictures, confronted by towering antlers or shooting rap-
ids in adroit canoes. I never actually saw much of this,
because I did not care to hunt and was not even very
keen on fishing, but I was taken, in the course of our
summers, not only to the inevitable Thousand Islands
but to Nova Scotia, Yarmouth and Halifax, to Quebec

37

and Montreal, and finally across the continent—stopping off at Winnipeg, Calgary, Banff and Victoria—on the Canadian Pacific Railway.

This last was in the summer of 1915, and I had not been in Canada since then till I returned about ten years ago to upstate Lewis County and again began spending my summers there. The call of the wild and remote is still, I am told by Canadians, often felt by American visitors. People even travel in planes to northern lakes which are otherwise difficult of access, and inexperienced tourists from the States sometimes turn up with skis in midsummer. But there is today a new kind of attraction: for example, the Stratford Festival, a mixed repertoire of theater and music, which takes place during two months of every summer in a little Ontario town. This is not very far from the United States border but is distinctly different from anything that we have in the United States. The productions there of Shakespeare and other classics, in the early years directed by Tyrone Guthrie, have had a brilliance and an originality that astonished one in contrast to Broadway, and between entertainments one can stroll in a trim bloom-embroidered park that reminds one of well-tended England.

I also visited for the first time Toronto, a rapidly growing industrial city, of which it is customary to say that it is getting to be indistinguishable from our similar cities in the Middle West but which I felt to have its own rhythm and accent. It is not, like Montreal and Quebec, particularly attractive in itself. The industrial part of Toronto has much of the crowding oppressiveness, and the business section much of the dreariness, if not quite the uniformity, of the Middle Western city in the States. The old residences of the Scotch Presbyterians who have, with the Methodists, constituted the dominant class are heavy, tight, forbidding fortresses which, though as a group they maintain their solidarity, seem each to have shut itself away from its neighbors. One feels that the windows of these houses are meant to be watched from, not seen into, and I am told that when the inmates hold festivities they always pull down the shades. The influence of Presbyterianism and Methodism has notoriously worked in Canada to discourage the practice of the arts and, except in the rather sporadic and sometimes brutish Scottish way, the enjoyment of the fleshly pleasures. Yet Toronto indulges itself today in lively night clubs and excellent restaurants. It possesses an immense new theater and a museum with a fine Oriental collection. It has a high-standard university, and it is the publishing center for English-speaking Canada.

It is evident that the rich Canadians, who have lately been getting richer, have finally reached the point, like our own millionaires by the end of the last century, of wanting to be patrons of the arts. They are endowing symphony orchestras and investing in modern paintings. The government, through the Canada Council, established in 1957, is subsidizing the arts, humanities and social sciences by a variety of grants, prizes and scholarships. The National Gallery, in Ottawa, has an excellently chosen selection of the work of first-rate sculptors and painters, recent artists as well as Old

Masters, including a collection made by the former Governor-General Vincent Massey, and it has been housed since 1961 in a new and modern building, in which the pictures are well hung and well lighted. The Canadian painters here, also, seem to appear to rather better advantage than in the more old-fashioned art museum in Montreal.

What impressed me most of all, however, was the fact that Canadian literature has recently become a good deal more interesting than I remember it to have been in my youth. I used to enjoy then the dialect versifying of William Henry Drummond, the James Whitcomb Riley of the French Canadian *habitant;* the bathetic Kiplingesque ballads of Robert W. Service, so suitable for convivial recitation; the quiet music of Bliss Carman's moods in the presence of an out-of-door world of yellow moonrises, golden waters, fresh meadow grass and fern-lined brooks, which never rises to lyrical dramatics; and the slapdash buffooneries of Stephen Leacock, which display a Canadian violence. One remembered, without ever having read them, the historical novels of Sir Gilbert Parker, which used to be seen on the shelves with the other historical novels of a shallow and shoddy period of manufactured American romance—a writer hardly now claimed by Canada, since he wrote most of his books in England, where he became a Member of Parliament and eventually achieved a baronetcy. But the work of Morley Callaghan and Hugh MacLennan, of André Langevin and Marie-Claire Blais, can take their places on a literary level far superior to any of these.

40

Toronto also differs from the States, in spite of much Americanization, in preserving a British tradition of good order and capable handling. You usually get better service at the airports and in the hotels, and the people in such public services are less hurried and more polite. Our panicky state of mind in the States—where we are threatened by apocalyptic war, ridden by intolerable taxes and eliminated by automation, where we suffer from insecurity of employment, incapacity for decisive opinion and uncertainty even of continued life—is reflected in both our dissipations and our outbreaks of irrational rioting and unmotivated homicide, in our administrative inconsistencies and in the messes we often make of our practical operations. In Canada, one gets the impression of less worry and more leisure. To a man of my generation, it seems closer to the old American world—though I imagine that the people of Canada, after withstanding their early ordeals, have always exerted themselves less and been less anxious about their enterprises than we in the United States. It is possible, in English Canada, to have reasonable conversations in which people pretty well speak their minds—they listen, I noted, to one another instead of "shooting off their faces" in competition, as we are likely to do—and the Canadians, as I shall show in a moment, now have subjects that stimulate discussion and about which we in the United States are in a state of almost opaque ignorance.

Yet I noticed in Canada, wherever I went, that the people in public places do not make room for one another but indifferently get into one another's way.

41

And the driving in Toronto is reckless to a degree that I have never seen elsewhere. It seems a series of narrow escapes. I was once thrown off my seat in a taxi driven by a young Chinese when a car in front suddenly stopped and he had to put on the brakes to avoid a crash. It was explained to me that the motorists were always playing "chicken." One driver will challenge another by refusing to give way before him: the game is to compel the other man to swerve or decrease his speed in order to avoid a collision. And on reflection I have come to the conclusion that these phenomena are to be explained in terms of an important difference between Canadian society and our own. This difference, as one western Canadian said to me, is that nobody in Canada is "melted." He was thinking of our "melting pot." It is a compartmented, not welded, community; that is, it is not really a community. The major compartmentalization—to which I shall return later—is, of course, between the French-speaking and the English-speaking inhabitants, but there are also many other compartments. The Canadians of Scottish extraction, with their parades led by kilted bagpipers and their ritual dancing of the Highland reel, have imposed on the whole of Canada their pronunciation of words like *about* as something not far from *aboot*, but they do not seem to mix much with anyone else. There is even a distinct difference between the Highlanders of lower Ontario and the Highlanders of Nova Scotia, where Gaelic is still sometimes spoken. Nova Scotia regards itself, in fact, as more or less a country in its own right, much closer to maritime New England than to the prosperous Scottish business world of Montreal. The Nova Scotians are likely to refer to the rest of the now rather misnamed "Dominion" as "Canada" or "Upper Canada." I am told that there is even on the island of Cape Breton a kind of Cape Breton nationalism which makes a distinction between its own inhabitants and the rest of the population of Nova Scotia. And then there are the immigrant populations: the Ukrainians, Poles, Russians and Icelanders, and more recently, in large numbers, the Hungarians and the southern Italians. These may still, after several generations, continue to speak their own languages. They are known as "the ethnics" or "the others," and I was told that the boast of the dominant English that these groups have been left to themselves, that no pressure has been brought to bear to assimilate them into the English-speaking culture, was a mask for official unwillingness to have them qualify for government jobs. There are also the Irish Catholics, who are not particularly friendly with the Catholic French, and the Ulstermen, with their once powerful Orange Order, who are always at war with the Catholics and who are not much beloved by the Scots. And even among French-speaking Canadians the Acadians make up a group that holds itself quite apart from the French of Quebec. Deported by the British in 1755, when the latter took over Nova Scotia, a good many came back later from New England. These have their own university and always speak of themselves as "Acadians." An Acadian, I was told, will not work for a Québecois French family. It may also be noted that one cannot

43

be sure that someone who bears a French name necessarily belongs to the French Catholic world. He may occupy a special position as the descendant of a Huguenot family which came over in the seventeenth century.

All these groups, then, exist side by side with very much less mingling with one another than would be likely to take place in the States. With us, there is the constant pressure to become "Americanized." But is there such a thing as being Canadianized? The Canadians have been debating in a rather academic way as to what it means to be a Canadian, without ever having been able to formulate a definition that is at all precise and that can be made to include everybody. And now the nationalist movement in French Canada is making this even more difficult. The British Dominion of Canada has never had a national flag—only the Red Ensign, as it is called, of the Canadian merchant marine, which has the Union Jack in the corner—while French Canada has employed as its emblem the flag of the Province of Quebec, a blue banner quartered by a thick white cross, with a fleur-de-lis in each corner. But now that British Canada's relation to England consists merely of belonging to the Commonwealth, an entity verbal rather than practical, and that the French Canadian nationalists are making it a point of honor to have a fleur-de-lis on their license plates, the new Liberal government of Lester Pearson is advocating a new, all-Canadian flag: three red maple leaves on a white background with—symbolizing the two oceans—a blue bar on either side. Mr. Pearson has not yet, as I write, been successful in getting Parliament to approve his new banner. This project has been blocked by the leader of the Conservative opposition, his predecessor, John G. Diefenbaker, who filibustered the debate for six weeks, until Pearson was reduced to entrusting the problem to a parliamentary committee. It is objected by Mr. Diefenbaker that this flag, being mainly white, would be easily soiled in summer and that in winter it would be almost invisible against the background of all-enveloping snow. It is also objected that white suggests the white flag of surrender, and that since the maple tree is hardly known in western Canada, the maple leaves would be inappropriate symbols. I noticed, on a recent visit, that in the Rosedale section of Toronto and in the Westmount section of Montreal the Union Jack was defiantly flown.* And there seems to have been a similar problem in regard to the national anthem. The French sing a song called *O Canada* and there is an English version of this, but the English have not always wanted to sing it. They have preferred *God Save the Queen* or *The Maple Leaf Forever*, which latter, on account of its reference to the defeat of Montcalm by Wolfe, is completely inacceptable to the French (they might also complain of the rhyming):

* Since this was written, Prime Minister Pearson has by closure put an end to the debate on the flag. The House of Commons, on December 15, 1964, by a vote of 163 to 78, approved the adoption of a new flag, though not the one described above. The committee to which the matter had been referred had proposed a different design: a single red maple leaf on white, with red bars instead of blue ones; and this is now to be the flag of Canada.

> In days of yore, from Britain's shore,
> Wolfe the dauntless hero came,
> And planted firm Britannia's flag
> On Canada's fair domain.

There seems now to be a general agreement that *O Canada* is to be sung.

This dissociation from one another of all these diverse Canadian groups may result in unfair exclusions and give rise to administrative difficulties, but to the visiting "American" it is rather a relief. There is conformity inside these groups of a sometimes constricting kind but no insistence on conforming to a national ideal which may become, as it has with us, all the cruder and less flexible for having to be applied to such heterogeneous material. The Canadian heterogeneity, unmolded, has at any rate made Montreal a cosmopolitan city of what seems to me a unique kind. Each group has its press and its restaurants and its places of entertainment. I found one man at a newsstand on St. Catherine Street—or, better, Rue Ste. Catherine—who spoke all the languages of the papers he sold, including Hungarian and modern Greek. And I was astonished to discover that Montreal, once the drab and crass provincial town that I vaguely remembered from my youth, had undoubtedly become one of the most attractive cities on the North American continent: smart shops, first-rate French restaurants, both better and less expensive than in New York, an excellent French theatre subsidized by the government, some gray old French streets that are being restored, innumerable steeples of churches, an old-fashioned and pleasant Ritz Hotel, a mammoth, supermetropolitan, overpowering new Queen Elizabeth Hotel, and the dominating "Royal Mount" that gives the city its commanding position above the immense St. Lawrence. There is also intellectual ferment to a degree that I had not expected. Eastern Canada is now perhaps more interesting than it has ever been before in its history, for it is going through a kind of triple crisis which cannot fail to affect its future and to give it perhaps a new role in North American civilization.

The three important issues in this crisis, I should state here, are briefly the following: (1) a struggle with the United States, which is primarily an industrial and financial but is also a moral struggle; (2) a struggle between French-speaking and English-speaking Canada, which has resulted, on the part of the former, in a movement for partial or complete independence; (3) a movement for drastic reform inside the Catholic Church, set off partly by the innovating policies of Pope John, partly by the death of Maurice Duplessis, for many years the Premier and boss of Quebec, which was followed by the immediate destruction of the political machine he controlled.

These notes are primarily to be occupied with the literature of contemporary Canada, but since this literature reflects all these issues and cannot fully be understood without some knowledge of Canadian history and the social and political questions which are now agitating Canada, it must lead to some discussion of these.

FRANCIS PARKMAN. The best way to lay a foundation for the understanding of Canada is to read Francis Parkman's great history, *France and England in North America*. I had supposed that I should find this unrivalled work, so fascinating as well as informative, a primary classic in Canada, and I was surprised not to see it in any of the bookstores or in the libraries of the houses I visited. I was even more astonished when a serious and otherwise well-posted young journalist told me that he had never heard of Parkman. But the reason for this became clear. Parkman had been banned by the Catholic Church, which did not want to have the historian's Protestant account of the methods of the Jesuits in converting the Indians (appreciative of their heroism though Parkman was), the bitter conflicts of the various religious orders and the ruthless machinations of Bishop Laval made accessible to its congregations. The Catholic university in Quebec, which is named after Bishop Laval, at one time entertained the idea of giving Parkman an honorary degree, then thought better of this idea, but Protestant McGill, in Montreal, did eventually give him one. It was suggested to me, too, by a French Canadian, that it was natural for French Canada, which so jealously bristles against English-speaking Canada and the United States, not to have wanted to have the best history of its early years written by an Anglo-American (though I found it asserted in some quarters that the best modern history of French Canada has been written by the American Mason Wade). British Canada, on its side, does not perhaps want to read so much about the exploits of the French in Canada. It seems astonishing to the American visitor that the first Canadian history which has attempted to deal comprehensively with the English and the French both and which aims at real objectivity should have been published only in 1946: the one-volume *Colony to Nation, A History of Canada,* by Professor Arthur R. M. Lower, of Queen's University, Kingston. In French schools, they have been teaching, it seems, only the history of the French in Canada; in British schools, only the history of the British. Of the official histories on either side, Professor Lower says that they "hardly seem to refer to the same country." So if the English-speaking foreigner has an interest in finding out how this queer situation arose and what is back of the tangential relations between Canada and the United States, he will do well to have recourse to Parkman.

At the time Parkman's history was appearing—the sixties, seventies, eighties and nineties of the last century—it presented itself as a project of an almost wholly novel kind. Parkman gave it as secondary title *A History of the American Forest,* and nobody had written before a chronicle of recent history which, instead of dealing almost exclusively with parliaments and chancellors and treaties, with organized armies and strategic wars, tried to follow the movements of white pioneers invading a continent of primitive peoples and unsurveyed wildernesses. No one in the United States had apparently been interested in this subject, had thought of it as an object for serious study. Such records of those times as survived had more or less the aspect of old debris in the back yard of American progress, of cherished family legends that might be handed down in the household but that nobody had had an interest in checking and relating to one another. But Parkman spent years of research among published and unpublished personal records, letters that had been somehow preserved yet never examined as evidence, state papers stowed away in the archives of London and Paris, the two Canadas and the United States.

In the immense panorama which he at last unrolled and to which he gave the rest of his life, he begins with the tiny groups of French Huguenots and Spanish adventurers continuing their wars of religion among uncharted waterways, unhealthy swamps and uncomprehended Indians. He then proceeds with the exploits of the Jesuits, enduring, much farther north, the extremes of torture and hardship; the exertions of La Salle and the other explorers—which in our day sound quite superhuman—in breaking through in the unknown West to the Illinois and the Mississippi; the founding by the French of the outposts that became Montreal and Quebec, attacked on the one hand by their murderous neighbors, the always undependable Indians, and hampered on the other by their difficult relations with the unimaginative authorities at home; the struggles with the English colonists for the forts on Lake George and Cape Breton; the grisly series of murders and burnings on solitary New England and Pennsylvania farms when the French, with their Indian allies, were systematically harassing the British. The historian concludes with the decisive battle for the mastery of North America when, in 1759, Wolfe vanquished Montcalm at Quebec and both died in a conflict of cultures which has not to this day been resolved.

How was it possible to construct a narrative which, never resorting to the methods of nineteenth-century romantic fiction, would carry along the reader through volume after volume, out of incidents and chains of events so scattered and disconnected, the doings of small settlements so isolated, the skirmishes and takings-of-possession so inconsecutive, sporadic and confused? One has to read about so many sieges, so many bleak and lethal marches, so many palavers with the Indians, so many spiteful intrigues for position among exiled and discontented colonial officials. The genius of Parkman is shown not only in his well controlled and steadily advancing prose but in his avoidance of generalizations, his economizing of abstract analysis, his sticking to concrete events. Each incident, each episode is different, each is particularized, each is presented, when possible, in sharply realistic detail, no matter how absurd or how homely, in terms of its human participants, its local background and its seasonal conditions. But a knowledge of all this could not wholly be drawn from the written sources, especially such inadequate documents as those with which Parkman had sometimes to work. He had already spent five months in the West, mostly living with the Sioux Indians, in order to get some first-hand knowledge of the peoples with whom the white men had at first had to share the continent, and he afterwards went to much trouble to travel to even the most distant sites of the happenings he had to describe—wild spots which were often still scarcely or not at all changed from the time when these events had taken place. He had a special sensitivity to landscape and terrain, a kind of genius unequalled, so far as I know, on the part of any other important historian, without which such a story could hardly have been told.

It was all right for the urban Gibbon to build up a description of Constantinople—and an extraordinary description it is, which even creates a kind of suspense —without ever having visited the city, but for America, as yet unconstructed, this method would never do. There were no models to follow for America. The historian must himself go to see what was seen for the first time by the immigrants. Lake George in winter: "In the morning they marched again, by icicled rocks and ice-bound waterfalls, mountains gray with naked woods and fir trees bowed down with snow. . . . When clouds hang low on the darkened mountains, and cold mists entangle themselves in the tops of the pines." In summer and autumn: "Embarked in whaleboats or birch canoes they glided under the silent moon or in the languid glare of a breathless August day when islands floated in dreamy haze, and the hot air was thick with odors of the pine; or in the bright October, when the jay screamed from the woods, squirrels gathered their winter hoard, and congregated blackbirds chattered farewell to their summer haunts; when gay mountains basked in light, maples dropped leaves of rustling gold, sumachs glowed like rubies under the dark green of the unchanging spruce, and mossed rocks with all their painted plumage lay double in the watery mirror." But it would take too many quotations to illustrate the variety of this master of prose: The desolate plains of the West, "half-covered with snow and strewn with the skulls and bones of buffalo"; Starved Rock, on the Illinois, from the trunk of whose "stunted cedar that leans forward from the brink, you may drop a plummet into the river below, where the cat-fish and the turtles may plainly be seen gliding over the wrinkled sands of the clear and shallow current"; the forests of Maine, dense and daunting—matted bushes, saplings choked to death, condemned by their very abundance. How he gives to this forest of Maine a teeming and tangled life quite distinct from that of any of his other forests! Yet he is scrupulous in never inventing. If some picturesque detail in Parkman may seem for a moment to be prompted by the fantasies of fictionalized history, you will find it is an actual impression recorded by one of his pioneers. (The contrast between Parkman's method and that of Professor Lower in the history mentioned above is significant of the development of Canada. Five hundred of the five hundred and sixty-one pages of Lower's distinguished book deal with events in that region after the point at which Parkman drops his narrative, and the chronicler, with expert skill, has spun a firm and even texture of the various gradually drawn strands that make subsequent Canadian history—the habits of social life, the modifications of political institutions, the conflicts of religious forces, the vicissitudes of immigration, the processes of industry, the shuttlings of trade and the ramifications of railroads in a Canada of average men, of stationary or migrating groups. Where Parkman would be vivid and specific, Mr. Lower may be found brief and vague. One would like to hear more about the incidents of such episodes as Papineau's rebellion of 1837 and Riel's later rebellions. Of the former, he tells us merely that "militarily, both sides behaved in the best traditions of comic opera," and in regard to the latter he gives us so little actual narrative that it is impossible to visualize what happened. I learn from an article in the *Atlantic Monthly*, by Mr. Douglas V. LePan, that Riel, as the head of his provincial government, was in the habit of receiving official visitors in moccasins and a frock coat—which Mr. LePan regards as illustrative of the incongruities of Canadian life. Parkman would have told us this, but Mr. Lower has undertaken to cover the very much more extensive ground of a less individualized story.)

The clarity, the momentum and the color of the first volumes of Parkman's narrative are among the most brilliant achievements of the writing of history as an art. After this, although his powers never fail him for presenting any aspect of his subject, the nature of the material itself occasionally obstructs the artist. In the middle of the step-by-step chronicle, the momentum a little flags. The French cities have by this time become big enough, with a society sufficiently developed, to demand the historian's analysis, and in the volume called *The Old Régime in Canada* he gives us this analysis at length; but these centers, in spite of their apings of the society of the old regime in France, are still rather meager and second-rate, and the rivalries and schemings and liaisons of the governors and priests and generals do become a trifle tedious when treated on a comparable scale with the more novel events that have gone before. One continues to read eagerly in order to find out what will happen to the white man adventuring in a world of whose inhabitants he has never before heard and whose geography he has still to discover; but the drawing rooms and convents of Montreal cannot excite an equal interest. And then Louisbourg—irreducible historical fact—is taken and retaken too many times; the sieges become rather monotonous. They may have bored Parkman, too, for—fearing that he might not live to finish his story—he skipped ahead to write the volume *Montcalm and Wolfe*, then returned to *A Half-Century of Conflict*. The suspense of the whole adventure, as an artistically created effect, is itself somewhat weakened by the explicitness of Parkman in telling us in his introduction exactly what the upshot is going to be and exactly what this upshot will prove. Not that he writes an obvious morality play; he never deals in heroes or villains. The objectivity that Parkman achieves is the product of a never-remitting discipline, which almost makes him lean over backward in admiring the nobility of the French, the chivalrous virtues of their soldiers and the grandiose ambitions of their leaders, and in rather playing down the more prosaic virtues of the New Englanders, Pennsylvanians and New Yorkers. But he has made it quite clear that the French, for all their visions and their efforts in this arduous new world, so different from anything they have known at home, are to be crushed "under the exactions of a grasping hierarchy," stifled "under the curbs and trappings of a feudal monarchy," whereas the Protestant English, already recalcitrant against their king and his church, "a busy multitude, each in his narrow circle toiling for himself, to gather competence or wealth," were in a position to build up independent industries and to establish enduring commonwealths. New France, though so far from home, had to suffer from the corruption of Old France, from its selfish inefficiency and extravagance, and it was let down by Louis XV when it most needed his help to survive. No ray of the Enlightenment reached it during the ferment of the eighteenth century; the revolution that overthrew the Bourbons and exalted the Goddess of Reason left French Canada Catholic and feudal, abandoned and yet unchanged. But New England was already the Revolution. It was bound to win against the British Tories, especially the second-rate officials who were usually sent out to the colonies. A good many of these fled to Canada, where they still had their Crown to back them, as the French no longer had theirs. Since most of this has already been told us at the very beginning of the story, the defeat of Montcalm by Wolfe comes as something of a Q.E.D.

The historical point being made—if we strip away the forests and the Indians—may then appear rather simple, and if Parkman does fall short in interest of the greatest of the European historians, such as Gibbon and Michelet, it is because he does not give us, cannot give us, in view of the limited resources with which his human materials provide him, the same sense of looking on at the whole destiny of Western man, of being made to confront man's great problems and to speculate as to what will be his future. Of course, Michelet and Gibbon cover many centuries, and they can range over the varied societies of a more or less civilized Europe, whereas Parkman extends over little more than two centuries and a half and deals mainly with a sparsely peopled wilderness. Yet the rough conflicts between small bands of men are significant because, though lost in this wilderness, they will eventually be seen to have contributed to the settling of important issues. One has somewhat to readjust one's sights to appreciate the drama of early America. The scale of humanity is so reduced, compared to that of denser societies, that it may not at once be obvious that great questions of Church or State may actually be at stake in a skirmish, a feud or a duel. And it is a history of such encounters that Parkman has written here. They may sometimes, in spite of all the scenery, appear to take place in a void, and we have by this time in the United States very largely lost the sense of that void. But one is aware of it again in Canada—looking out, for example, from the Île d'Orléans, in the St. Lawrence just above Quebec. From a high cliff, the wide smooth river and its flat opposite bank are of a magnitude quite dumfounding. There are no bathers along the banks; there are, they say, no proper beaches, and the water is rather dangerous. Such a prospect seems annulling to human assertion, which can hope to make so little impression in that hemless hardly peopled continuum of water and land and sky. How can one get a hold on such a country? It would especially not lend itself to painting. What need can one have of pictures, surrounded with such a view, and how could a frame contain it? Music? Its vibrations would be lost in the void. And literature? Can one think of such spaces in terms of any human meaning? And yet there are scattered dwellings along the opposite shore, and it is punctuated by one sharp steeple. The steeples that prick from these shores— more frequent as we approach Quebec City—give the landscape its human value. And so do the books written here—the voices that seem sometimes as far apart as the farms and the camps and the cities, that do not even always communicate with one another, since there never appears until recently, with the exception of a few small groups, to have been anything like a "literary life" in Canada. The French and the English writers do not often read one another, nor do writers who belong to the same language group necessarily read one another; they may, in fact, not even know of one another's existence. Yet there seem to be more and more of these voices, and they are becoming more penetrating. From their fables and their lyrics and their essays, it is evident that Canadian writers, in their relative isolation, are, like their ancestors the first settlers, taking stands now and making decisions which will influence the future of their country.

———

HUGH MACLENNAN. It is easy to pass from Parkman to Hugh MacLennan—another writer strongly to be recommended to anyone who wants to understand Canada—for Mr. MacLennan shares with Parkman the historical and geographical imagination. Hugh Mac-Lennan is so special a figure that he requires some explanation. I should describe him as a Highlander first; a patriotic Nova Scotian second (he is a native of Cape Breton); a spokesman for Canada third; and—but simultaneously with all of these—a scholar of international culture and a man of the great world. After Hugh MacLennan's graduation from Dalhousie College in Halifax, he went to Oxford as a Rhodes Scholar, then got a Ph.D. at the Princeton Graduate School, at both of which places he specialized in classics. He has taught in schools and colleges in Canada and has visited France and the Soviet Union.

I first became interested in MacLennan when I read his book of essays, *Scotchman's Return*, published in 1960, and found in it a point of view surprisingly and agreeably different from anything else I knew in English. MacLennan writes here, as in his other books of essays—*Cross-Country* (1949) and *Thirty and Three* (1954)—with much humor and shrewd intelligence about Canada, Scotland, England, the Soviet Union and the United States. I came to recognize that there

59

did now exist a Canadian way of looking at things which had little in common with either the "American" or the British colonial one and which has achieved a self-confident detachment in regard to the rest of the world. A good many of these essays form a chronicle of the process by which the author arrived at the Canadian point of view that he has brought to so sharp a focus. It was developed in the course of encounters with the people of other nationalities, which stimulated on his part, when he returned from abroad, a new interest in his native country. He gives us, in *Thirty and Three*, a curious account of one of these experiences. He had apparently, as a Nova Scotian, known little of the rest of Canada. But, "The first week I was in Oxford . . . an English freshman invited me to tea. He began to talk about Canada and was amazed to discover that I knew nothing whatever about my own country. I had never heard of Timmins [in Ontario, the largest gold-mining town in Canada], I had never spent hours and hours in a train rolling across the shield of northern Ontario. I had never seen the drama of dawn rising over Manitoba, or the sun setting behind the Continental Divide, or the moon over Georgia Strait. But this young Englishman had seen all these things and more. He had seen them because an organization in England had made plans to enable youngsters to do so and had put the plans into effect by raising the necessary cash."

When MacLennan got back to Canada, he set out to educate himself, and this resulted in a series of novels that are as solid and analytic as the essays are informal and personal. Before going on to consider these novels, I want, however, to indicate some of the features of Mr. MacLennan's specifically Canadian point of view as it is expressed in both his essays and his fiction. The problem for this type of independent mind is, on the one hand, to shake off the traditional ties that have in the past bound the Canadian to old England and, on the other, to survive the pressures that have been driving him toward the new United States. In Mr. MacLennan's first novel, *Barometer Rising*, published in 1941 and laid in 1917, the more intelligent characters are chafing against the first of these relationships: "And Halifax, more than most towns, seemed governed by a fate she neither made nor understood, for it was her birthright to serve the English in time of war and to sleep neglected when there was peace. It was a bondage Halifax had no thought of escaping because it was the only life she had ever known; but to Murray this seemed a pity, for the town figured more largely in the calamities of the British Empire than in its prosperities, and never seemed to become truly North American." . . . "Living in a great nation virtually guaranteed by the United States, the present crop of publicists seemed determined to convince Canadians that their happiness would be lost forever if they should aspire to anything higher than a position in the butler's pantry of the British Empire." . . . "There was Geoffrey Wain, the descendant of military colonists who had remained essentially a colonist himself, never really believing that anything above the second rate could exist in Canada, a man who had not thought it necessary to lick the boots of the English but had merely taken it for granted that they mattered and Canadians didn't."

I am told that there are few such old loyalists left. The independence of the Canadian Parliament was established by the Statute of Westminster in 1931. In 1935, the giving of Canadian titles was abolished, and an attempt was even made to have the old titles extinguished. In 1949, the Canadians agreed to dispense with "the right of the subject to lay his case at the foot of the throne"—that, is to take it to London and submit it to the Judicial Committee of the Privy Council, who were not likely to know much about Canada or be much concerned about what happened there. The attentions of British royalties are no longer, even by the English Canadians, received with the enthusiasm they once were. The recent visit of the Queen and her consort provoked hostile demonstrations on the part of the French nationalists and required a bodyguard of five thousand troops, police and Mounties. It is true that the British North America Act, which was passed in 1867, when the provinces confederated, and which serves Canada as a constitution, is a statute of the British Parliament and cannot be amended except through Westminster, but definite steps are now being taken to "bring the Constitution home."

As for Canada's relations with the United States, the acquisition by American capital of some fifty per cent of Canadian industry has provoked, in certain quarters, to outspoken hostility an antipathy which has always existed, and this hostility is increased among people of taste by the ever-increasing addiction of the popular audience to our popular entertainment: magazines, movies and jazz. In the case of our magazines, the Canadian publishers have the serious grievance that, by bringing out special Canadian editions, such periodicals as *Time* and the *Reader's Digest* divert from the Canadian magazines a good part of the national advertizing, without which it is impossible for them to get along, and measures are now under discussion to keep Canadian advertizing at home. It was partly by taking a stand against absorption by the United States that Diefenbaker became Prime Minister and managed to remain in office from 1957 to 1963. There was a very strong opposition to our demands to build airbases in Canada. If the United States, said the Canadians, has been so stupid as to commit itself to nuclear weapons on a scale that could annihilate whole countries, why should Canadians, on this account, allow us to involve them, too, in the dangers of nuclear warfare? (Mr. Pearson has, however, capitulated, and we have now two Bomarc missile bases in Canada.) Our own official version of our methods and intentions does not necessarily go down in Canada, and Hugh MacLennan was expressing himself as follows not long after the last war: "When the Japs bombed Pearl Harbor and the Germans followed it up with a declaration of war, I knew the Americans were going to be hard. All their righteous horror at the bombing of cities done by other nations would disappear. I knew that they were going to bomb hell out of Germany and Japan, that they were going to wage war with loathing for its traditional aspects of infantry marches and travel in strange countries, but with a cold fascination for what they could do technically, and that engineers would work miracles now that they had the government money behind them. I knew that the whole nation would come together and find itself, and in spite of the war be happier than it had been in the 1930's. I knew the Americans were going to display a ruthlessness—not crude, personal savagery hand to hand, but a mechanical and distant ruthlessness—which would make what Hitler and Tojo had in mind seem like something out of the Middle Ages." "The Americans were bound to do something like that one day," says the heroine of MacLennan's novel *The Precipice* (published in 1948), when she hears the news of Hiroshima.

The Precipice, which is made to take place partly in the United States, is of great interest to an "American" reader. A young American businessman carries off from a little Ontario town a sweet but very proper and family-ridden girl who has not found any local boy at once worthy of her and capable of breaking down her defenses. The young man gets a job in an advertizing agency, and they go to live first in New York, then in Princeton, from which he commutes. They have two children. Their marriage collapses. The husband, committed to the pace of New York and to the meretricious work he is doing, has come more and more to depend on the acceleration of Scotches and Martinis. He takes up with a sophisticated career girl, and eventually he ceases to come home at all. "Alone

MAKING AN HONEST WOMAN OF HER?

Duncan Macpherson: Lester Pearson and John G. Diefenbaker. *Courtesy of the Toronto* Daily Star with the children in Princeton, Lucy began to wonder if one of the causes of her failure to hold Stephen's love might not simply be the fact that he was an American and she was not. . . . Had she as a Canadian, raised in a small country which once had believed the United Kingdom to be the center of the world, failed to understand what this terrific spectacle of rising American power meant to someone like Stephen Lassiter? A man could be conscious of it without being a politician. The sense of this power was everywhere. During the depression it had slept like a hibernating animal grunting and tossing in its cave, but now it was striding forth, darting its eyes backward and all around, insensately loud and proud in exact proportion to its haunting knowledge that the greater it grew the more certain it was to lose forever the freshness of its youth and the very innocence which has made America unique." Lucy later on explains to one of the Canadian characters the situation of the United States at the end of the war: "The other night after we heard about the atomic bomb I began to think of the Americans the way you do—like a great mass of people and not as individuals. I saw them moving in a vast swarm over a plain. They had gone faster and farther than any people had ever gone before. Each day for years they had measured out the distance they'd advanced. They were trained to believe there was nothing any of them had to do but keep on travelling in the same way. And then suddenly they were brought up short at the edge of a precipice which hadn't been marked on the map."

Stephen loses his job, goes to pieces and disappears. The author attributes his fall to the frustrating efforts of the old-line Americans to make up for the loss of their religious discipline and of the toughness of the early industrialists by the excitements of unrestrained sex and of frantic commercial success in a world of clever women and sharpers. Lucy returns to Ontario, but she does not revert, as the reader is at one moment led to expect, to a ne'er-do-well admirer of her youth. She finally locates Stephen and salvages what is left of him. She has thrown in her lot with energetic America rather than with lethargic Canada, and now that Stephen has smashed up she will stick with him.

These quotations may suggest that MacLennan is unsympathetic to both England and the United States, and, though critical of the weaknesses of Canadians, he does sometimes like to allow them to score; but he is by no means unappreciative of the qualities of other English-speaking peoples. His essay in *Scotchman's Return* called *The Curtain Falls on the Grand Style* is at once a sort of epitaph after Suez and a tribute to British character. He ascribes the success of the English to a capacity for utter recklessness carried off by a brazen arrogance combined with an offhand manner.

The misgivings of contemporary Canada in regard to its position in the world are recorded in *Barometer Rising*. The conviction that the country has at last matured as an organic national entity appears in MacLennan's most recent novel, *The Watch That Ends the Night* (1959). This story takes place during the

Second World War. "Strange years," the narrator comments, "which now have become a blur. While the war thundered on, Canada unnoticed grew into a nation at last. This cautious country, which had always done more than she had promised, had always endured in silence while others reaped the glory—now she became alive and to us within her excitingly so. My work brought me close to the heart of this changing land. And sometimes, thinking with shame of the Thirties when nothing in Canada had seemed interesting unless it resembled something in England or the States, I even persuaded myself that here I had found the thing larger than myself to which I could belong." It is interesting to discover that Professor Lower, in his history mentioned above, expresses a similar opinion: "There was slowly coming to people," he says, "the consciousness of their own identity. They were slowly discovering the fact of their own existence and were even beginning to believe that there was some merit and value in being Canadian."

What I have said will provide the coördinates for locating the nationalism of Hugh MacLennan. Having taken up his post as observer and critic, he has set out to render in his fiction some systematic dramatization of the life of eastern Canada; but it ought to be said at this point that the topical interest of his subjects does not always coincide with the literary interest of his novels. If the work of Morley Callaghan has some kinship with that of Turgenev and Chekhov, Hugh Mac-Lennan is of the school of Balzac, and, like Balzac, he is extremely uneven. The novels of Mr. Callaghan almost always involve moral problems; they are made to take place in Canada, though the locality is sometimes not even mentioned, but they do not concentrate on Canada: they are studies in human relations. Mr. MacLennan seems to aim, on the other hand, to qualify, like Balzac, as the "secretary of society," and one feels that in his earnest and ambitious attempt to cover his large self-assignment he sometimes embarks upon themes which he believes to be socially important but which do not really much excite his imagination. An example of this, it seems to me, is his probably best-known novel, *Two Solitudes* (1945). The subject here *is* important. There is no question that the estrangement in Canada of the French and the British from one another, their antagonism and mutual incomprehension, have constituted a baffling obstacle to the development of Canada as an entity. The visitor from the melting pot is astonished to be told by members of each of these linguistic groups that it has been possible in Canada to grow into one's teens hardly knowing that the other group existed. French and British may meet to talk business, but they have almost no social life in common, and I was informed in Toronto by a Scottish observer that the top people in Montreal would not utter a word of French or allow their children to learn any. A French Canadian said to me that in the English universities the students might take several years of French, learning the grammar as if it were Latin, and not be able to order dinner in a French restaurant in Montreal. I found that there were exceptions to this, though only among exceptionally cultivated people, and that McGill University, in Montreal, has instituted intensive French courses. But one does detect a certain snootiness in the attitude toward the French of the British Montrealers—the kind of attitude that the British have always adopted toward the natives of British colonies or the inhabitants of countries they are occupying. The French reciprocate this attitude—they like to think of the British as barbarians— and they extend it to the United States, about which they seem to make a point of knowing as little as possible. Events in the United States are given the front page in English Canadian newspapers but are reported only scantily in the French. French Canada has never got over the battle of the Plains of Abraham—in which, one French Canadian said to me, "we are told that we were defeated"—and an American Northerner who is well aware that the Southerners are still rallying around Robert E. Lee and refighting the Battle of Gettysburg in such a way as to make it come out differently may nevertheless be surprised to find that the surrender of 1760 is still rankling in the Province of Quebec, and that the French in Montreal, who outnumber the British three to one, still refer to them as "*les anglais*" or "the garrison."

I shall return to this situation later, but it has been necessary to mention it here because this novel of Hugh MacLennan's has especially attracted attention— was, in fact, when first published, a sensation—on account of an unprecedented boldness in taking this bull by the horns, and the fact that its title—the "two solitudes" are those of the two mutually exclusive groups—has now become a common phrase seems to demonstrate that Mr. MacLennan has contributed to a realization on the part of English-speaking Canada that social solitude to that degree may not be entirely desirable. Yet, as a novel, to a reader from the States, *Two Solitudes* rather affects one in the same way as those schematized works of fiction of the period after the Civil War which tried to dramatize the problems of Reconstruction or, in the early years of this century, the relations between capital and labor. Mr. MacLennan, as a social satirist, is amusing when he writes about rich Montrealers entertaining a visiting Englishman, but although he does his honest best with the household, so rustic and antiquated, of Athanase Tallard, the French seigneur, one feels that this has not been experienced as imaginative fiction should be.

Another book by Hugh MacLennan that does not seem to me successful is *Each Man's Son* (1951). Here one guesses that it must have occurred to him that he ought to do something about Calvinism, so depressing and hampering an influence on the mind of Presbyterian Canada, but one feels that the relationships and the mental crises which he contrives to illustrate this influence have, in the same way, not really been lived by the author. It is not that I object to the introduction in Mr. MacLennan's novels of disquisitions on politics, religion and society. Although H. G. Wells and his school are now very much out of favor, there are, after all, a good many people who occupy themselves seriously with these matters and who feel, think and talk about them, but in certain of Mr. MacLennan's novels the ideas have not always been incorporated as organic elements of the drama.*

And now, having got out of the way what I regard as two artistic duds, let me go on to an appreciation of what I regard as Mr. MacLennan's achievements. If he is dull when he is merely being conscientious, he is capable, when an emotional force lays hold of him and charges his material, of enveloping the reader in a spell that makes it hard for one to separate oneself from the story. I found this true of both *The Precipice* and *The Watch That Ends the Night*. Two of the passages best executed in these—invested with a kind of poetry that, to a reader in the United States, makes Canada seem almost exotic—are, in the former, the life of the three orphaned sisters in the slow-paced Ontario town, with its loneliness and its comforts, its adjustments and its tightening tensions, and, in the second, the escape of the strong-minded boy from the lumber camp in which his mother has been murdered by her lover, when he navigates an unknown river, alone in a stolen canoe. This spell of Hugh MacLennan's is of rather a

* Mr. MacLennan writes me that *Each Man's Son* "was not written to attack or even to emphasize Calvinism," but that the Boston publishers insisted upon his adding the introduction which gives this impression, on the ground that "without it the underlying motivation of the story would be incomprehensible to an American audience." He did so, he says, with reluctance but has omitted this introduction from a later paperback edition. It still seems to me that this novel has been *willed* rather than lived. It is curious, but characteristic of our assumption of the remoteness of Canada, that any such explanation should have been thought to be necessary—and, of all things, an explanation of Calvinism in of all places, Boston.

71

special old-fashioned kind that we do not often find in modern fiction. He is quite right to emphasize his Highland background, because he has a strong strain of the romantic Scot, and he sometimes echoes the cadences of Robert Louis Stevenson, sometimes conveys the excitement of Walter Scott. It has been said of him that he now and then lapses into the spirit of the women's magazines, but I believe that on these occasions he is simply surrendering himself to a Scotchman's melodramatic sentiment: "Douglas, Douglas, tender and true," Roderick Dhu and the lovely Ellen. This has evidently a Highland source; but he derives from Presbyterianism the compulsive passages of preaching which occasionally interrupt his narrative. He may carry you through almost a whole book—as in *The Watch That Ends the Night*—by the power of poetic vision, then let you down at the end in a spasm of revelation that will leave you disappointed because unconvinced. I think that the trouble here is that he finds a certain difficulty in ending his novels because—unlike Morley Callaghan—he cannot bear to leave his characters, always exposed to possibilities of disaster, without some positive salvation and exaltation. His books are full of moral reawakenings. No matter how despairing one has been, one must pick oneself up in good order and not merely face life again but ride on in a gallant spirit. One's honor is of paramount importance; one must never be trapped into actions that are unworthy of a man of honor: "I had come there hating her. I had come remembering Catherine and prepared to say anything to make her leave

72

Jerome [Catherine's husband] alone." . . . "Norah Blackwell really was lethally attractive, and I was attracted to her myself, and under the circumstances I hated myself for being so." Nothing could be further than this from the moral tone of recent fiction. I am writing this not long after seeing the stage version made by J. B. Priestley from Iris Murdoch's novel *A Severed Head*, in which everyone goes to bed with everyone else with a facility that completely leaves out of account any question of fidelity or propriety. On the stage this is very funny, but I find it a relief in MacLennan to read about some decent women who are capable of lasting affection—because such women do exist, and MacLennan has described them in a way which is appreciative without ceasing to be realistic. The heroine, Catherine, of *The Watch That Ends the Night*, is hardly a satisfactory character; she is supposed to inspire adoration, yet we do not feel we know what she is really like. But Penelope Wain, in *Barometer Rising*, with her job in the offices of the shipyards and her background of heavy respectability, capable, loyal, inexpressive and obstinately independent, is a perfectly convincing picture of one type of Canadian girl, as is Lucy Cameron in *The Precipice*, drawing back from the New York delirium for reliance on the straightness and stability that have been bred in her by her native Ontario town, with its somewhat stodgy middle-class conventions. The success of these characters is due to their having been firmly grasped as women, to their not having been, like Catherine, somewhat blurred and made insubstantial by a befuddlement of romanticization which may, in this case, have been hard to avoid, since the story is told in the first person and the narrator remains in love with her all his life.

Hugh MacLennan's methods as a novelist are usually as old-fashioned as the virtues of his characters. The beginning of *Two Solitudes* reminds one of the opening of *Ivanhoe:* "The sun was setting upon one of the rich grassy glades of that forest, which we have mentioned in the beginning of the chapter. Hundreds of broad-headed, short-stemmed, wide-branched oaks, which had witnessed perhaps the stately march of the Roman soldiery, flung their gnarled arms over a thick carpet of the most delicious greensward. . . . The human figures which completed this landscape were in number two, partaking, in their dress and appearance, of that wild and rustic character, which belonged to the woodlands of the West-Riding of Yorkshire at that early period. The eldest of these men had a stern, savage, and wild aspect. His garment was of the simplest form imaginable," etc. In *Two Solitudes*, after the opening pages of description, it is Père Beaubien the parish priest and Athanase Tallard the seigneur, instead of Gurth the swineherd and Wamba the jester, who take up a good many pages of landscape and social background as a setting for a very brief conversation. It can never have occurred to MacLennan that beginning a book in this way is likely to discourage the modern reader. In an essay called *The Story of a Novel*, in which he describes the writing of *The Watch That Ends the Night*, he explains that after

Hugh MacLennan. *Photograph by Sam Tata*

putting down "millions of words" and tearing up "again and again . . . I refined my style and discovered new techniques I had previously known nothing about." But when one comes to the novel, it is hard to see what he means by "new techniques," except that the story is told partly, by a now pretty familiar device, in a series of flashbacks that alternate with the narrative of the later happenings. The one feature of Mac-Lennan's novels that does seem to me new and interesting is his use of the geographical and the meteorological setting. He always shows us how the characters are situated—as they pursue their intrigues, undergo their ordeals or are driven by their desperate loves—in a vast expanse of land and water, the hardly inhabited spaces of the waste upper margin of a continent. We are sometimes even told where they are in respect to the heavenly bodies. Halifax: "The sky was bright with stars. Orion and Sirius stood over the forest, and the Bear, stretching a long arm to the northwest, rested above the Basin. The forest was hushed on the verge of winter storms, and the Basin, walled by darkness and illuminated by the stars, seemed filled to capacity with ships awaiting convoy. Their riding-lights flickered like a swarm of fireflies motionless in a void." In the Laurentians: "Sipping our drinks we looked out over the lake which now was heavily shadowed along the length of its western shore with the promontories thrusting their outlines far out and deep down, the sun still bright but westerly over the hills. The wind had dropped and in the total silence of the empty north land we heard the musical sigh of a tiny stream coursing through the trees into the lake. Apart from the sound of the stream this stillness in which we sat went all the way north to the Arctic and all the way west to Hudson Bay. A robin swooped down to settle on a patch of manured ground and stood listening for worms." If it is windy, we are likely to be told exactly where the wind is coming from: "The Cameron house was so dark that lights had to be turned on during the day and a wind that had started far down the Mississippi Valley and then had been pushed eastward by a cold front moving from Hudson Bay tore over the rolling Ontario land." It is true that the people of Canada, widely scattered and with their rugged climate, are more conscious of geography and weather than we usually are in the United States, but one feels that Mr. MacLennan goes a little too far in attributing to one of his women an awareness of geography as vivid as his own: "The car whispered along quietly and once Lucy had the sensation of being at rest while the landscape shifted and flowed past. She pictured the waterway stretching from back eastward along the trail of the *voyageurs* to the point where Lake Ontario ends and the St. Lawrence begins, through the flat land of Dundas County where lighted ships in the canals seem like long, low houses moving across the darkness of the fields, through the blaze of light at Montreal and thence down the avenue of the river past the intimate lights of parish after parish, past Quebec and the Île d'Orléans till the river widens into the solitudes of salt water and no lights remain, and the air is cold and surges smash and drag in the darkness along the empty cliffs of the Gaspé and Labrador."

This last is, however, a good example of Mr. Mac-
Lennan's style at its best. This style is subject at moments to the same sort of lapses as the tone of his
dramas. He is capable of beginning a chapter as follows: "So that summer I entered Arcadia and the pipes
played and the glory of the Lord shone round about."
Or of making a man speak like this in a moment of
strong emotion: "I love you, Lucy. I can do anything
now. I can trample down everything that's kept me
back. It's been inside me, that's where the trouble was.
I love you, Lucy." It is easy to pick out these banal-
ities. I am sorry that, simply by quotation, it is impossible to show how excellent Mr. MacLennan's
writing can be when he is carried along by the sweep
of one of his large descriptions or impassioned actions
that are solidly realistic and yet never without their
poetry. The most sustained example of this is his first
novel, *Barometer Rising*, which deals with what might
seem the unpromising subject of the great Halifax
disaster at the time of the First World War, when a
small French ship loaded with munitions collided with
another ship and the explosion devastated a whole city.
I find this also, although less ambitious, less brilliant
and less surcharged with emotion than some of Mr.
MacLennan's other novels, still perhaps his most completely satisfactory performance. You hardly feel the
personality of the author, much in evidence in his
identification with some of the characters of his other
books. He seems to have incorporated himself in the
city of Halifax. The story covers only eight days,

which are recounted hour by hour, and Mr. MacLennan appears to know every street and what everybody in the streets is up to, in a way that one would think would have impressed Arnold Bennett. But he imparts to the life of this prosaic city an excitement of suppressed suspense that one hardly finds in Bennett. One follows, as in the Wandering Rocks chapter of *Ulysses* —from which book I suspect he has learned one new technical trick, though he says he could never read it through—the varied and sometimes disjunct characters going about their various errands in different parts of the city. Where will the explosion find them? Who will be killed? Who survive? How will it affect their relationships, bring to a climax the strained situations? The description of the explosion, when it comes, is, I daresay, one of the best things of its kind in fiction. It seems plain that Mr. MacLennan must have had some first-hand knowledge of these events, but I was astonished, when I looked him up, to discover that he was nine at the time. The imagination here for locality, for urban construction, for shipping surely reaches the point of genius. But this is not merely the documented naturalism that my account of it, I am afraid, is bound to suggest; the book is the work of a powerful poet who has mastered the materials of the engineer.

There is also a parable in *Barometer Rising*, but not preached about or allowed to grow maudlin, as in some of his other novels. Here Canada is already in the First World War, rather reluctant to be dragged over to Europe for the purpose of defending Britain. The soldiers are uneasy and skeptical, and yet vaguely loyal to England. The businessmen are all for the war, since the war industries are giving them the chance to put themselves almost in a class with the big operators of American business. But the time is coming soon when Canada must for the first time achieve self-consciousness as a nation. It will be jolted into independence by this brutal intrusion from the outside world, this involvement in faraway conflicts which should be none of the Canadians' immediate business and which yet can cause their destruction not only in those distant countries but even on their own shores. The wounded war veteran from Nova Scotia who has been wandering about Halifax homeless, disgraced by the false representations of an ambitious shipping magnate who has been his superior officer and who has used him, thinking him dead, to cover up a mistake of his own, survives and is vindicated while the magnate is found crushed by the rubble, in bed with his secretary. This is melodrama, to be sure, as the author, writing later about the book, confesses. (He likes to have his Nova Scotians assert their sterling maritime qualities in opposition to the sordid practices of the worldlings and the promoters of the industrial cities.) But that hardly makes the book less authentic. I find in it the intense interest of a hitherto unexploited subject—the intimate social life of Canada, studied seriously and accurately described by an intelligent and gifted writer. It seems to me that *Barometer Rising* should not merely be accepted, as it is, as a landmark in Canadian writing but also, as an artistic success, be regarded as one of its authentic classics.

———

THE FUGITIVE. One of the most interesting of the younger Canadian novelists is John Buell of Montreal. He has published two novels—*The Pyx* and *Four Days*. The first of these is a horror story—a shocker, and an extremely effective one. The principal character is a high-class call girl who finds herself caught in the toils of the Montreal underworld and condemned to some dangerous and degrading ordeal of the hideousness of which she is warned but of the nature of which she knows nothing. It is not really a serious book, but it creates an ever-tightening apprehension that may hold even a reader not particularly susceptible to the coils of this kind of fiction.

Four Days, though we are still in the underworld, is an effort on a higher level, a narrative equally full of suspense that is also a psychological study. A young boy who lives with a criminal brother, to whom he is abjectly devoted, is made use of by this brother as the ideal confederate to get away with the swag from a bank robbery. He is told to take a bus to a certain town and to stay in a certain hotel, and his brother will meet him there. He is to say that he is waiting for his uncle to bring him to summer camp, and he has been promised that he will actually be sent to one. The robbery takes place and the money is passed to the boy, who carries it away in the bag that he uses for delivering papers; but the police have been tipped off, and in a skirmish with them the brother is shot to death. The boy has seen him collapsed in the street, but tries to believe that he has not been killed. He proceeds to the country hotel, and the rest of the book consists of the chronicle, hour by hour, of his agonized waiting there for the brother who will never appear. He reads in the paper that his brother is dead but is unable to face this situation, which leaves him with nowhere to go. The story is technically less adroit than *The Pyx*; the author breaks up the main narrative, which follows the adventures of the boy, with some rather perfunctory melodramatic scenes that explain what went wrong with the robbery and other matters which the boy cannot know, but there is created here a different kind of horror: the boredom, full of foreboding, which tries the reader with its long delay, of the dreary Canadian town, in which the boy walks back and forth along the same roads; of the shoddy country hotel, in which he feels he is under suspicion, alone with nothing left in the world except the bag with the stolen money and a long jackknife which his brother has given him and with which he has eventually to defend himself by sticking it into the neck of a sympathetic homosexual who has offered him refuge in his camp in the woods but has wanted to exact a price.

The flight of the boy from this camp reminds one of the flight from the lumber camp of the boy in Hugh MacLennan's *Watch*, and actually what we have here in the experience of the innocent boy criminal is recognizable as the latest variation on one of the recurrent themes of modern Canadian fiction: the fugitive who is running away from justice, from some dangerous pursuer or from organized society itself. I have spoken of the instinct of "Americans" to renew their eroded self-confidence, their conviction of primitive strength, by betaking themselves to Canada. In Canada itself, also, the men like to leave their communities and to get away to the wilds: it is still a part of their pride that they are able to face these wilds and survive. Is the life of respectable cities—and no cities could ostensibly be more respectable than Toronto, Montreal and Quebec—often felt as a confinement, a burden? It may be an outlaw like Kip Caley, in Morley Callaghan's *More Joy in Heaven*, who, released from prison for good behavior and taken up as a pet by the moneyed classes, is caught back by his underworld connections and again commits a deed of violence, to be hunted down and shot by the police—or any other of Mr. Callaghan's several principal characters who find themselves at odds with society; or any one of the several wanderers in the novels of Hugh MacLennan, who return to but do not belong in a tight busy civic organism, who have to recognize that their instincts are quite out of tune with the correctitude they had left behind. Whether they plunge into the underworld or the hinterland, they are trying to get away. In *Four Days*, the orphaned boy, carrying out the instructions of his outlawed brother, is to find himself exiled in both. In the fiction of French Canada we shall meet again these disaffected or frightened fugitives who, with very rare exceptions, are frustrated or finally extinguished. In connection with French Canada, however, it is enough for the present to point out that in both the French society and the British you have a formidable and rigid church which stands for the status quo and which, by its very nature, is bound to drive the more audacious spirits to condemn themselves to a blind antagonism. This instinct to escape may derive from the original seceding impulse that spurred the ancestors of both kinds of Canadians to take the risks of departing from Europe. In the New World, this impulse persisted. Why not, they would feel, in this boundless new land, go farther and depart from the settlement? In French Canada, the *coureurs de bois* were moved to evade the constraints of even their still very crude civilization. Once released in the forest, they would drop all pretense of respecting its conventions and regulations, and they would sometimes go to live with the Indians. It is partly, I believe, this pattern which persists into modern Canada and which furnishes these themes for Canadian fiction.

John Buell would make a good bridge for a transition to French Canada from British. He is bilingual (his mother was French); he says that he thinks of *The Pyx* as essentially a French novel, and *Four Days* has been translated in France. He is thus in the curious position, probably possible only for a Canadian, of writing in the English language excellent novels which he regards as essentially French but which are published in New York and Paris and little known in either French or British Canada.

But I want to make a pause at this point to offer some explanation of the purpose and scope of these notes. I do not want it to be supposed that I am attempting here an adequate survey of even current Canadian literature, or of even, necessarily, the best of this. I have not tried to be comprehensive, and it may well be thought that my subjects have been chosen rather arbitrarily. There are writers I have not read—such as Robertson Davies and Ethel Wilson, Ringuet and Yves Thériault—who I am told are of special interest, and I hope that I shall not be reproached for omitting these figures or others. I am not pretending here to do more than try to call attention to some writers who have attracted my own attention. My ignorance of the subject is still immense. I have hardly touched the West Coast at all, and I come to the contemporary French writers knowing little about their predecessors. I find that an encyclopedic volume, *Littérature Canadienne-Française*, by Samuel Baillargeon, lists articles on ninety writers, from the earliest explorers up to the nineteen-sixties, and this does not include any writers who have appeared since 1960.* The last

* A new edition of a book by Professor Gérard Tougas of the University of British Columbia, *Histoire de la Littérature Canadienne-Française*, is more up to date than Baillargeon. Professor Tougas speaks, in his preface to this 1964 edition, of the problems of perspective raised for him by "four years (1959-1963) of an intense literary activity." He notes in passing that Baillargeon, a priest, is rather prone to condemning writers on the ground of "*déviationsime morale.*" This is true, but I cannot see that it much affects his literary judgments. To the foreigner, both books are useful. Baillargeon's is a schematized textbook—which has, however, the advantage of illustrations; Tougas, though academic, represents a more personal point of view.

84

twenty years or so in French Canada have evidently been more prolific in literature than any period that has preceded them, and there are now, I am told, more titles being published in French-speaking than in English-speaking Canada, though, of course, more Canadian English books are published in the United States than Canadian French books in France. *Creative Writing in Canada*, by Desmond Pacey, the English counterpart of Baillargeon, first published in 1952 but now, in a new edition, brought up to 1961, discusses also dozens of writers of whom the non-Canadian will never have heard.

———

POETRY. It seems to me that the poetry of Canada, both in French and in English, is on the whole less interesting than its fiction. You can find a representative section in the recent *Oxford Book of Canadian Verse*, compiled by Mr. A. J. M. Smith. One of the merits of this excellent anthology is that it includes both English and French. It is, indeed, the first anthology to do so since a single much earlier one, now out of print and out of date, and, together with the appearance of *Canadian Literature*, a bilingual quarterly edited by George Woodcock and published by the University of British Columbia, it is evidence of a cultural *entente cordiale* that is evidently quite new in Canada. The pieces in the *Oxford Book* have been exceptionally well selected—Mr. Smith is himself a poet —and the synoptic introduction is illuminating. What is attractive in the earlier Canadian poets is that they are never ambitious professionals. They are settlers who from time to time have been moved by the raw landscape or by their arduous lives to express themselves vividly in verse. I am thinking of such pieces as Standish O'Grady's amusing *Old Nick in Sorel* (Old Nick was compelled to recognize that he could not stand the winters there), and *The Canadian Herd-boy*, by Susanna Moodie: this herdboy, and this herdboy alone, knows the path to the grazing ground of the cattle; through the dark swamp he threads and the "tangled maze of cedar boughs"; the jingling of the bells sounds more clearly.

> He sees them now; beneath yon trees
> His motley herd recline at ease;
> With lazy pace and sullen stare
> They slowly leave their shady lair;
> Cobos! Cobos! far up the dell
> Quick jingling comes the cattle-bell.

These early poets are sometimes grim, like Alexander McLachlan:

> We live in a rickety house,
> In a dirty dismal street,
> Where the naked hide from day,
> And thieves and drunkards meet.

> And pious folks with their tracts,
> When our dens they enter in,
> They point to our shirtless backs,
> As the fruits of beer and gin.

The hard Canadian winter has its moments of strenuous jollity, as in the *Sugaring* described by Pamphile Lemay:

86

> Les chemins sont durcis comme par le rouleau,
> Et la lune les montre en des éclairs de glaive.
> La neige des tapis, que nul vent ne soulève,
> Donne une teinte chaste au sylvestre tableau.

But the huge caldron is boiling, the maple sap is flowing into the trough, the tin bowls are waiting in the cabin on the table without a cloth, and if the boys and girls get to nibbling at the maple crystals together, somebody will surely get kissed.

These Englishmen and Irishmen and Scotchmen will sometimes attempt long performances on historical and geographical subjects in their traditional blank verse or Spenserian stanzas; the French, in their alexandrines, which ring strangely, as if with no echoes—so far from the resonant platforms of Lamartine and Victor Hugo —in the wastes of those *"quelques arpents de neige"* which Voltaire thought were no great loss when Louis XV let them go at the Peace of Paris. But one of these French poems has a special historical interest for the foreigner as well as for the French Canadian. *Le Drapeau de Carillon*, by Octave Crémazie, written in the middle of the last century, has long been a piece that French Canadian schoolchildren have been made to memorize, and it provides a kind of simple key to the whole situation of French Canada:

> Pensez-vous quelquefois à ces temps glorieux,
> Où seuls, abandonnés par la France leur mère,
> Nos aïeux défendaient son nom victorieux
> Et voyaient devant eux fuir l'armée étrangère?

Though "abandoned by their mother France," the French Canadians were still fighting the English; they had taken Fort Carillon, and their flag-bearer, returning from the war, had cherished the white flag that was the emblem of victory. When Montcalm had, however, been beaten by the English, the old soldiers, on Sundays after Mass, would rally at this poor man's cottage and revive their heroic memories. The veteran conceives the idea of making a trip to France and going to the King with his banner. He will tell him what disasters they have suffered, what sacrifices they have made, and he will beg him to send them the help which, when they had needed it most, he withheld. He carries out his project of going to France, but at Versailles he never gets past the courtiers, who know nothing about Canada and laugh at him. Only a few old soldiers condole with him. The poet denounces the King for the extravagance of his vices and Voltaire for his infidelity and his never-forgiven phrase. The veteran returns to Canada and, unable to bring himself to tell the truth to his old companions in arms, assures them that the King has promised to provide them with reinforcements. But when they next come to visit him, they find him gone. He has taken the old flag and returned to the battlefield, and there, with his banner spread over him, he is found by peasants, a frozen corpse. The poet apostrophizes the flag and exhorts the French Canadians to be loyal to it, "to defend from every attack their language and their faith." This poem, for all its old-fashioned rhetoric, I find extremely moving. What differentiates it from most other patriotic ballads is that it tells of tragic defeat and offers no hope of reprisal.

The poetry of the later nineteenth century runs to often attractive landscapes—by Sir Charles G. D. Roberts, Bliss Carman, Albert Lozeau—and one continues to find such landscapes in the poetry of the twentieth century. Mr. Pacey, in his *Creative Writing in Canada*, quotes two poems which make a piquant contrast—one by Marjorie Pickthall:

> Wind-silvered willows hedge the stream,
> And all within is hushed and cool.
> The water, in an endless dream,
> Goes sliding down from pool to pool
> And every pool a sapphire is
> From shadowy deep to sunlit edge,
> Ribboned around with irises
> And cleft with emerald spears of sedge. . . .

And one by A. J. M. Smith:

> Cedar and jagged fir
> uplift sharp barbs
> against the gray
> and cloud-piled sky;
> and in the bay
> blown spume and windrift
> and thin, bitter spray
> snap
> at the whirling sky;
> and the pine trees
> lean one way. . . .

The best of these landscapes, however, are probably those of Albert Lozeau, who was immobilized at eighteen by ankylosis and who occupied himself in writing descriptions of what he could see from his window. He laments in one of his poems that he can never know the lakes and mountains of Canada. His love poems are tender and rather dim, those of an invalid made wistful by a woman's kindness, but he is exquisite when he is writing of the sound of wind, of the effects of hoarfrost and snow, of the maple turning red in autumn or losing its now yellow leaves. Here are some lines on the moonlight, with a marvellous effect produced by frozen *m*'s and liquid *l*'s:

> Ces soirs-là, comparant l'ombre qui rôde en lui
> A la blanche splendeur des choses de la nuit,
> Le poète isolé du monde, dans sa chambre,
> Rêve à la grande paix des tombes de décembre
> Et du linceul d'hermine amoncelé sans bruit
> Qui, sous le ciel empli de clair de lune, luit.

It is better perhaps, however, to read Albert Lozeau in anthologies than to go to his collected poems, because the record of these natural phenomena is bound to become monotonous and eventually a little insipid. But his *Épilogue* to his lifework is touching, with a pathos like that of Milton on his blindness. He is most moving, it seems to me, here and in the following poem, in which he sighs over his unfulfillment:

> J'attends. Le vent gémit. Le soir vient. L'heure sonne.
> Mon cœur impatient s'émeut. Rien ni personne.
> J'attends, les yeux fermés pour ne pas voir le temps
> Passer en déployant les ténèbres. J'attends.
> Cédant au sommeil dont la quiétude tente,
> J'ai passé cette nuit en un rêve d'attente.
> Le jour est apparu baigné d'or pourpre et vif,
> Comme hier, comme avant, mon cœur bat attentif.
> Et je suis énervé d'attendre, sans comprendre,
> Comme hier et demain, ce que je puis attendre.
> J'interroge mon cœur, qui ne répond pas bien . . .
> Ah! qu'il est douloureux d'attendre toujours—rien!

When one comes to contemporary English verse, as one reads it in Mr. Smith's selection, one finds later poets who *are* ambitious and who sometimes, in comparison with their predecessors, may seem nothing short of prismatic. But here again, when one reads them in quantity, they are likely to prove disappointing. They are all, one finds, fearfully imitative—of Eliot, Yeats, Auden and especially of William Carlos Williams and Ezra Pound. Louis Dudek, the son of Polish parents, and Irving Layton, born in Rumania, have performed a very useful function by getting rid of Presbyterian inhibitions and by suddenly, in British Canada, once so sober in its manners and dress, breaking out in harlequin coats that announce their cosmopolitanism, and they and others have been able to maintain magazines which have given Canadian poets an opportunity of publishing their work without depending on the literary market. But, though audacious and full of high spirits, the voices they raise are not very arresting, and they are likely to depend too much on those cadences of the early nineteen hundreds which are not very far from prose and upon which it took Ezra Pound, by his sharp and laconic phrases, to impose the true stamp of poetry, and on the homely, non-musical droning of William Carlos Williams (who gave high praise to Irving Layton). They seem to think that they have done what is necessary when they have ended some impression or reflection with one of those dying falls to which Pound gives ironic point but which here have too often the accent of mere mechanical echoes. The monthly *Canadian Forum* prints pages of poems of this kind, which might almost all be written by the same person. And when Canadian poets are satirical, they sound mostly like undergraduates being irreverent in the college magazines. Mr. Smith and Mr. F. R. Scott have collected examples of this humorous verse in a volume called *The Blasted Pine: An Anthology of Satire, Invective and Disrespectful Verse.* But you have to be bitter for this kind of thing, and it is difficult for an English Canadian to find anything to be bitter about. Mr. Scott tries his hand at a satirical poem on the long-time Prime Minister Mackenzie King. But how can one be bitter about Mackenzie King? What is baffling about Canadian Prime Ministers is their powerlessness, in general, to do anything dynamic or striking. They are so much kept suspended in a void between the gravitational pulls of the various groups, who live in different parts of the country, belong to different cultural traditions and represent different economic interests, that it is difficult for them to lay down clear lines, to make publicly avowed decisions. This widely scattered conflict of constituencies must either result in inaction or be smoothed over by a policy of compromise. It is for this that Mr. F. R. Scott is ridiculing Mackenzie King, and the result, though no doubt to the point, is less an incisive satire than a political editorial:

W.L.M.K.

How shall we speak of Canada,
Mackenzie King dead?
The Mother's boy in the lonely room
With his dog, his medium and his ruins?

He blunted us.

We had no shape
Because he never took sides,
And no sides
Because he never allowed them to take shape.

He skilfully avoided what was wrong
Without saying what was right,
And never let his on the one hand
Know what his on the other hand was doing.

The height of his ambition
Was to pile a Parliamentary Committee on a Royal
  Commission.
To have "conscription if necessary
But not necessarily conscription,"
To let Parliament decide—
Later.

Postpone, postpone, abstain.

Only one thread was certain:
After World War I
Business as usual,
After World War II
Orderly decontrol.
Always he led us back to where we were before.

He seemed to be in the centre
Because we had no centre,
No vision
To pierce the smoke-screen of his politics.

Truly he will be remembered
Wherever men honour ingenuity,
Ambiguity, inactivity, and political longevity.

Let us raise up a temple
To the cult of mediocrity,
Do nothing by halves
Which can be done by quarters.

In the English Canadian world, it is only—as far as my experience goes—in the cartoons of Mr. Duncan Macpherson that one finds a high level of political satire. These appear in the Toronto *Star*, but they go far beyond the editorial. They are the work of a vigorous imagination which, taking its cues from political events, expands them into gratuitous fantasies. Macpherson *is* bitter on the subject of war and on Canada's yielding to the United States in the acceptance of nuclear bases, as in his picture of the skeleton-whore —"Gotta match?"—soliciting under a monument "To Our Glorious Dead." But in his caricatures of the personalities of Canadian public life he has created a phantasmagoria for which the mediocre subjects themselves sometimes seem hardly adequate. Former Premier Diefenbaker becomes animated with an energy that is truly demonic, and the Canadian common man, undersized, gopher-nosed and chinless, is surrounded by predatory monsters who bewilder him, bully him, rob him, and are likely to leave him in tatters. The version of foreign affairs could only be that of a Canadian—see Macpherson's amusing cartoons on the relations between Kennedy, Khrushchyov and Castro—and is thus of particular interest to the non-Canadian inquirer; but these drawings, of which three albums have been published by the *Star*, have a value not confined to their aptness as a day-to-day political commentary. The cartoons of David Low were thus limited; they will have their historical importance as a clear and quizzical record of the political events of half a century. But Macpherson's, like those of James Gillray, may be fas-

Duncan Macpherson: John G. Diefenbaker turning into De Gaulle. *Courtesy of the Toronto* Daily Star cinating quite independently of our interest in or knowledge of the happenings they commemorate. Macpherson is a Gillray reduced in scale, a more scaring and grotesque Lewis Carroll. I do not doubt that the originals of his drawings will hang someday in Canadian galleries.

————————

E. J. PRATT. There are among the poets, however, two writers—one English, one French—who, I think, should be brought to the attention of the non-Canadian world. E. J. Pratt, who died recently at the age of eighty-one, had written an immense amount—an edition of his collected poems runs to almost four hundred tall pages —and he came to be revered in British Canada as the patriarch of its poetry. Canadian critics sometimes wonder why he is hardly known anywhere else, but this question is easily answered. When a reader in the United States or England picks up the huge volume of Pratt, he is confronted with a great many long narrative poems and by shorter poems that are also rather long and that cannot readily be picked up from the page. In these shorter pieces the poet is rarely at his best, and he does not lend himself to being anthologized. As Professor Northrop Frye says in his introduction to this collected volume, Pratt has to be read in bulk. But when the reader habituated to modern verse tries to come to grips with one of Pratt's long pieces, he finds himself following meters that take him back to Byron and Scott, with a phrasing as little polished and a rhythm that verges sometimes on doggerel. What carries all this off, however, is the natural verve of the poet and the rush of his narrative power, which sometimes rise to splendid eloquence and strike off delightful imagery. These merits, though quite individual, are also of rather an old-fashioned kind—the felicities of the poet in spate, who does not care about delicate craftsmanship. Pratt's recklessness, together with his imagination, when it runs to humor and fantasy, reminds one of *The Ingoldsby Legends*, Hogg's *Kilmeny*, and the legends of Praed, and in that kind of performance this poet can be sometimes extremely effective. One hardly notices the roughness of the metrics; one hardly pays attention to the rhymes, which, though often very clever ones, seem to have come to the poet's fingers without his thinking about them. (He is not so successful in blank verse, where it is easy for the careless to become prosaic.) And his vocabulary has also this readiness to acquit itself in any situation; his admixture with the traditionally literary of the technical and the scientific has often surprising results.

Pratt's subjects, though presented with considerable realism, are likely to be grandiose: a great disaster like the sinking of the Titanic or an heroic event like the retreat from Dunkirk, the ordeals of the Jesuit missionaries among the American Indians or the driving of the last spike of the Canadian Pacific railroad. Even his humorous poems are cosmic—a supersaturnalia of witches, which is made to involve all the spirits of the earth and the underworld; a terrible prehistoric war between the land and the water creatures. Pratt was born in Newfoundland and, like MacLennan, he is always conscious of infinite forbidding spaces. In the midst of all this wind and water, these sweeping elemental forces, it is difficult to attain intensity, and in his tumultuousness he is sometimes clumsy. But his kind of imagination has its grandeur and its catastrophic drama, and it could only have been stimulated to such imagery by the materials provided by Canada. It has the freedom of a supernatural as well as a natural world that lies far beyond human habitations; it ventures into unknown domains where it can only encounter wild animals or Indian warriors who seem equally wild; it moves over the immensity and uncertainty of the sea, which can always obliterate its trespassers, and beneath the far constellations, which we have made the attempt to domesticate by naming them for earthly shapes and for mythological figures, but the challenges of both of which abysses move man to augment his energy, to widen the scope of his work, and to heighten his human stature.

ÉMILE NELLIGAN. This poet is at once the Rimbaud and the Gérard de Nerval of French Canada, and he seems to me the only really first-rate Canadian poet, French or English, that I have yet read. Émile Nelligan's mother was French, but his father had come over from Ireland. At school, the boy did poorly and failed to finish, yet his vocation as a poet was passionate and from his earliest years all-absorbing. His first poems were published when he was sixteen, in 1896, and he was soon the star of an École Littéraire in his native Montreal. He read all the then modern poets, and his work shows a variety of influences: Baudelaire, Verlaine, Heredia. But he developed his own rich imagery and his own perfection of form, which make him, in the Canada of the end of the century, a quite unfamiliar phenomenon. He has nothing of the dilution and tepidity which were encouraged in the United States by the slack standards of our magazines. All his poems are full of point and close-packed; some are very complex. A virtuosity of meter, rhyme and assonance, a peculiar intensity and strength make something that is Nelligan's own out of even the Verlainean pathos or the metallic Heredian sonnet. In this poetry of stained glass, golden heavens and dawns that bathe the mountains in blood, of celestial visions as dazzling as the luxury of fabrics and gems, one almost loses sight of the milieu in which these brilliant pieces were created, and yet the chill sternness of that milieu lies behind these bright tapestries, in the background; it is suggested by the recurrent rhyme *givre-vivre*, which reminds one of the recurrent problem of survival in that paralyzing climate, and by the glimpses of family life, in which even the mother's piano, by whose music the boy is enchanted, cannot make him forget the lace curtains, the faded brocade and moire, all the dreary *"mobilier de deuil,"* by which he finds himself surrounded. A poem of six lines strikes the note:

De mon berceau d'enfant j'ai fait l'autre berceau
Où ma Muse s'endort dans des trilles d'oiseau,
Ma Muse en robe blanche, Ô ma toute maîtresse!
Oyez nos baisers d'or aux grands soirs familiers . . .
Mais chut! j'entends déjà la mégère Détresse
À notre seuil faisant craquer ses noirs souliers!

He speaks often of his *"névrose"*—once it is *"mes troupeaux de névroses."* Nor are his visions of madness mere exercises: the idiot woman who wants to find the church bells in order to hold them in her hands, the "spectral bull," huge and red, *"aux cornes glauques,"* "from which we must all flee." He had said to one of his friends, *"Je mourrai fou comme Baudelaire."* The *coup de grâce* seems to have been given him when his charming poem *Le Perroquet* was criticized by a visiting French journalist at a meeting of l'École Littéraire. At a subsequent meeting of this circle at the end of May, 1899, he recited *La Romance du Vin*, which involved a retort to this critic:

C'est le règne du rire amer et de la rage
De se savoir poète et l'objet du mépris,
De se savoir un cœur et de n'être compris
Que par le clair de lune et les grands soirs d'orage!

But he declares that he is full of gaiety and celebrates the ecstasy of his drunkenness.

Serait-ce que je suis enfin heureux de vivre;
Enfin mon cœur est-il guéri d'avoir aimé?
Les cloches ont chanté; le vent du soir odore . . .
Et pendant que le vin ruisselle à joyeux flots,
Je suis si gai, si gai, dans mon rire sonore,
Oh! si gai, que j'ai peur d'éclater en sanglots!

One of the audience reported that *"les applaudissements prirent la fureur d'une ovation,"* and his comrades carried him home on their shoulders. Two months later, he was found kneeling and reciting his poems before a statue of the Virgin. He

99

was evidently schizophrenic, and he spent the rest of his life in an institution. Under pressure of a constant struggle with a practical prosaic father who wanted him to be a clerk, he had been desperately concentrating his forces on preparing a volume of verse, which he did not retain his faculties to put into final shape. After his moment of public triumph, he suddenly short-circuited, burnt out and, tragically, became indifferent. For the reader, to come to the end of Nelligan's exciting poetry and to learn of the blankness that followed is like learning of the last years of Nizhinsky:

> J'ai la douceur, j'ai la tristesse et je suis seul
> Et le monde est pour moi comme quelque linceul
> Immense d'où soudain par des causes étranges
>
> J'aurai surgi mal mort dans un vertige fou
> Pour murmurer tout bas des musiques aux Anges
> Pour après m'en aller puis mourir dans mon trou.

But he lived on till almost 1942. He had published in periodicals, at the time of his extinction, no more than twenty-six pieces, but his reputation was kept alive, and there were several editions of his poems. On the occasion of the third edition, there was a radio reading of his poetry, to which the poet himself, it is said, listened "*d'une oreille distraite.*" It was, however, only in 1952 that Nelligan was done full justice, with a scholarly *Poésies Complètes* in the series called Collection du Nénuphar, which included a good many pieces thitherto uncollected. It would seem that, as in the case of Hopkins, his original editor was rather afraid of some of Nelligan's more *délirantes* pieces, which were likely to be disconcerting to the conventional taste of the time. Of certain such poems only fragments survive, one of which had been cited by this editor as the kind of thing that was not worth saving. French Canadian literature was long to remain at least fifty years behind Paris.

2

CRITICISM. One does sometimes find able reviewing in Canada, but in general the situation in this department may appear to the outsider provincial. The critics seem very uncertain of themselves. They are inclined either to overpraise Canadian books or to be afraid to praise them. This latter is partly due no doubt to their feeling that they lack authority, which they assume to reside in England, in the United States or in France, and do not want to risk sticking their necks out; but partly, too, I am afraid, because literary mediocrity is predisposed to be spiteful to talent. If mediocrities are given real power, as they are in the Soviet Union, where hack writers become officials who can censor and suppress their betters, the effects may be crippling or annihilating. We had at one time in the United States—at the beginning of the last century —a situation somewhat similar to that of Canada at the present time. When James Fenimore Cooper, for example, had become a popular novelist in England and on the Continent, his books were received at home not merely with disparagement but with venomous hate.

The reviewers, still unsure of America, seemed to regard it as a kind of impertinence that an American should be well received abroad and that his books should lead the readers of the Old World to presume to dictate to Americans which of their products they ought to applaud.

I provoked a striking example of this reaction when I wrote the first piece in this book in appreciation of Morley Callaghan's novels. Instead of helping his reputation in Canada, this seemed to arouse fury. Professor F. W. Watt of Toronto University, in a review of one of Callaghan's books, referred—though ironically —to the indignation aroused by "the effrontery of this Yankee imperialism." I wondered, why "Yankee imperialism," and, on inquiry, I was given to understand that the accepted opinion in Canada was that Callaghan could write short stories but was incapable of writing novels, and that they resented my praising these latter. I was thus, from their point of view, trying to dispose of Canadian property in the same way that other Americans had done when they bought up Canadian industries or recommended to the Canadian government the policies that our government would prefer. When I asked one of the younger novelists to account for the annoyance I had caused, he replied that I must understand that to be an artist in Canada was regarded as "a kind of sin, and to be a good artist makes it worse." In talking to another young novelist, a woman, I told her how Sartre and Cocteau had got Jean Genet out of prison, to which he had been consigned as a thief, by appealing to the authorities on the ground that he was the best French writer of his generation, and I added that in no country but France would it be possible for an habitual criminal to be liberated on such a plea. She remarked that in Quebec it was the other way. If anyone had told the authorities there that someone was the best writer of his generation, that writer would have been put in jail. The young man writes English and the young woman French, but both the French and the English writers in Canada have been up against social groups that are in principle hostile to literature. The Scottish bourgeoisie of the cities believe that the chief aim in life is to work very hard and make money, and that an artist is a weakling and a trifler; if he devotes all his time to his work, he becomes one of the very worst things that it is possible to be in British Canada —a man without a regular job. The Church in French Canada, on its side, fears literature as a possibly subversive force, which may make people impatient of authority and of the meager education they have been getting.

But this grim situation is relaxing. One can gauge it in French Canada by the bookshops. Henry James, after a visit to Canada in 1871, wrote of Quebec that it "must be a city of gossip; for evidently it is not a city of culture. A glance at the few booksellers' windows gives evidence of this. A few Catholic statuettes and prints, two or three Catholic publications, a festoon or so of rosaries, a volume of Lamartine, a supply of ink and matches, form the principal stock." Octave Crémazie, the patriotic poet I have quoted above, went bankrupt when he opened a bookshop in Quebec with the intention of bringing to the Québecois all the latest publications from Paris. Today there are well-stocked French bookstores in both Quebec and Montreal, offering everything from Voltaire to Genet. I was told that it was sometimes possible for the priesthood to bully a bookseller into refusing to carry a Canadian book that was thought to be deleterious to its interests. But the prominent display in these shops of the works of the philosopher-paleontologist Pierre Teilhard de Chardin, the very publication of which was forbidden by Rome during his lifetime, is a sign of emancipation.

And today, both in French and in English, a real criticism—that is, a criticism by Canadians of the products of their own culture—is beginning to crystallize. Encouraging evidences of this are two paperback anthologies compiled by Mr. A. J. M. Smith with the same sure taste and intelligence that he brought to the *Oxford Book of Canadian Verse: Masks of Poetry* and *Masks of Fiction*, in the New Canadian Library series. The first sentences of the editor's introduction to the former of these collections are a warning against one of the tendencies on the part of Canadian criticism that I have mentioned above: "To overpraise the native product in literature or to adopt a special standard in judging Canadian books is the mark of immaturity, in the critic or reviewer as well as in the literature that seems to need such encouragement. Today the avoidance of this temptation or, better still, the inability to feel it as a temptation at all is the mark of the seriousness, intelligence, and usefulness of a literary critic in

Canada." Most of the authors of the essays assembled here do try to live up to this, but in the volume of essays on poetry we find Professor Northrop Frye, in a postscript to a series of letters in which he had undertaken, from 1952 to 1960, to report on new Canadian poetry, confessing that he has adopted deliberately the policy of estimating this literature not in "world but in Canadian proportions. . . . I have for the most part discussed Canadian poets as though no other contemporary poets were available for Canadian readers."

French equivalents to these recent essays collected by Mr. Smith may be found in French or bilingual periodicals—especially the studies in *Cité Libre* by Mlle Jeanne Lapointe, who teaches literature at Laval University, and the papers collected in the volume called *Une Littérature Qui Se Fait* by M. Gilles Marcotte, who has done regular reviewing in the Montreal press. A group of essays called *Convergences*, by M. Jean Le Moyne, contains a somewhat exacerbated criticism of French Canadian society and of French Canadian literature as a reflection of this society. M. Le Moyne is a good deal harder on his section of literary Canada than most of Mr. Smith's critics are on theirs. The French, he says, ought not to delude themselves that, when looked at in "the global perspective," their literature is of any real importance. "It is to me extremely disagreeable to announce that my frequentation of the world of French Canadian literature is to a great extent a matter of profession and duty; that I do not find much there to nourish me and that I usually dine badly on it. I should add that it would be perfectly possible for me never to revisit that world and yet not to be deprived of any indispensable aliment."

This line of thought takes him to the roots of what he believes to be wrong with French Canadian society. The opinions expressed in his book are provoked by the acute double crisis through which that society is passing, and we must try now to understand the conflicts that have produced this crisis. Let us commence by considering an explosive book, a polemic from inside the Church, which has lately been more widely read and more excitedly discussed in French Canada than the work of any novelist or poet.

———

"LES INSOLENCES DU FRÈRE UNTEL." In October, 1959, M. André Laurendeau, the editor of *Le Devoir*, a "liberal" Montreal paper, received a long letter from a young lay brother, a teacher in a remote country parish, which complained of the badness of the education in French Canadian schools. Laurendeau got the writer's permission to publish this letter in the paper and invented the pseudonym le Frère Untel—Brother So-and-So. (The real name was Jean-Paul Desbiens.) This letter was followed by others, which criticized the Church in Canada with a bold and sometimes brutal wit. The writer was obviously a man of intelligence and ample reading. The material of these letters was later incorporated in a small book, published, in 1960, with the title *Les Insolences du Frère Untel*, with a caricature on the cover—rather misleading because vulgarizing—of a cassocked monk grinning ferociously as he kicks away an old tin can with an enormous black-booted foot. This book has been a major sensation. In French Canada, nothing like it had ever been known. My copy, purchased two years and a half ago, says "a hundred and eighteen thousand," and the book has even been translated into English under the title *The Impertinences of Brother Anonymous*, and has attracted some attention in British Canada.

Le Frère Untel begins his attack with a description of the French spoken in Canada. This language had already been designated by M. Laurendeau as *"le parler joual,"* because *cheval* in French Canada has been deformed to *joual*. It now involves so many special expressions that it has even been found worthwhile to compile a *Petit Dictionnaire du 'Joual' au Français*. Of the vagueness of the schoolchildren in their knowledge of French, le Frère Untel gives startling examples from the attempts of his pupils to write down from dictation the French version of the anthem *Ô Canada*:

> Ô Canada, terre de nos aïeux,
> Ton front est ceint de fleurons glorieux.
> Car ton bras sait porter l'épée,
> Il sait porter la croix.
> Ton histoire est une épopée
> Des plus brillants exploits.
> Et ta valeur, de foi trempée,
> Protégera nos foyers et nos droits.

Here are some of the versions of this submitted by students of from eight to eleven years' schooling:

111

Au Canada
Taire
de nos ailleux

{
Ton front est sein
ton front est sain
ton front essaim de fleurons
ton front est sein de flocons
}

{
De fleurs en glorieux
et fleuri glorieux
de fleurs en orieux
}

{
Quand on passe
car nos pas
quand qu'on part
quand on pense
}
car ton corps, c'est porter l'épée
Il s'est porté la croix

{
Ton histoire est une épépée
ton histoire est tu épopée
}
des plus brillants espoirs
Et cavaleurs

{
de froid trempé
de voir trembler
de foi tremper
de foie trempler
de voix tremblé
de foie trempé
de foi tremblée
de foie tremblay [Tremblay in French
Canada is a common family name.]
}

This demonstrates, says le Frère Untel, not merely appalling illiteracy but a neglect of "patriotic and civic" instruction. In the past, public education in French Canada has been exclusively in the hands of the clergy, and to attack the Department of Education was therefore to attack the Canadian Church, but this does not prevent le Frère Untel from giving voice to what is evidently a long-pent-up exasperation. "The crisis of any system of education—and especially in the case of Quebec—is a crisis of the teachers themselves. The teachers do not know anything, and they hardly know that they don't know. (It's not by expressing such amiable opinions that I'm going to make friends and succeed in life.) They must all of them be sent to school. For two years. After that, we could open up shop again." Any appeals to the heads of the Department are messages to Humpty Dumpty's fish. His recommendations for dealing with them are as follows: "I have, of course, a tender heart. I do not want to give pain to anybody. The Department must be closed down. So I propose that all of the members of the Department of Public Education be decorated with all the existing medals, including the medal for Agricultural Merit; that there even be created some special medals—as, for example, a medal for Solemn Mediocrity; that we guarantee to all these people a comfortable and well-paid retreat and then send them home to their mamas. That would turn out to be cheaper than paying them to complicate our existence, as is the case at the present time."

And as for the teachers themselves, with the Catholic universities behind them, what is to be expected of them? Le Frère Untel is a graduate of Laval, and Laval, he says, has had its good men, but the Faculty of Philosophy there does not meet its responsibilities. The professors hardly ever write anything, and when they do they write so badly that they might just as well not have written. "Their excuse is that to write down thought is to materialize it too much. This, it seems, is one of the reasons that Jesus Christ never wrote anything. It is true that the master of all of them, Monsieur Saint Thomas Aquinas, has written a tremendous lot. But, precisely, that's enough for them that Thomas wrote. They are content now to make commentaries on the writings of Thomas—when they are not making commentaries on the commentaries: the cube root of Saint Thomas." They are completely out of touch with the contemporary world. They are supposed to be experts in philosophy. Yet isn't it in the name of a philosophy that fourteen million Russians are in pickle in Siberia? (Le Frère Untel himself, as not infrequently happens in French Canada, was a little behind in his history.) Wasn't it in the name of a philosophy that six million Jews were gassed? "During all the time we studied with that Faculty, there existed very few courses that touched upon contemporary problems and the realities of life in Canada. They never found any way of connecting with actual life the universal principles with which they flirted. We were getting our degree at a time when a general crisis in education was going on: forums, panels, student strikes and all the rest. But not a single word of en-

Le Frère Untel, with his students. *Photograph by René Bénard* lightenment ever reached the Rue Sainte-Famille, where Sophia [the Greek word for Wisdom, Knowledge] still executes every day the graceful and harmless movements of her metaphysical exercises, the little trollop! From time to time, they made a pretense of fencing a little with Bertrand Russell or Bergson or Maritain, but it was all too plain that our musketeers were aware that they were well out of reach of Bertrand Russell's foil. If no Existentialist thinking is going on in the Faculty of Philosophy, is it any wonder that none is coming from anywhere else?"

He goes on to accuse the clergy of discouraging the people with religion. "We are terribly afraid of authority; we live in a bewitched atmosphere in which we feel that it is a matter of life or death not to infringe any taboo, to respect all the formulas, all the conformities. The diffused fear in which we live sterilizes all our activities." But "nothing that oppresses is Christian. Christianity is essentially liberating." And authority is crushing the world; there are very few free men left. We churchmen like to talk about liberty, but what we really want is security.

Le Frère Untel was, of course, himself savagely attacked. But it turned out that many people—especially among the young—had been thinking what le Frère Untel was saying. He includes a long letter from a nun who is also a teacher and who complains that in the Canadian convents they are not allowed to take advantage of the educational programs on television, and that since a nun is never allowed to go anywhere without being chaperoned by another nun, even in answering the telephone in a distant wing of the convent, it is impossible for her to take a university course unless there is at least one other nun registering for the same course. Their young pupils are told that they must live up to an ideal of "pride, purity, joy and victory," and "la Sœur Une Telle" believes that they do pretty well with purity, but how can they achieve pride, joy and victory "when their hands are tied, their hearts all swollen with unrealizable dreams, their eyes riveted to the dead inspirations of formalism"? The young, she says, are growing impatient. I have certainly, in talking to young French Canadians, found as much impatience with their Church as with the treatment of them by the English. As soon as I began making visits to French Canada some years ago, I began hearing about "anticlericalism." I at first assumed that this anticlericalism was of that already well-known kind which dates from the eighteenth century: that of the non-believer who attacks and exposes the priesthood. But I discovered that it was an anticlericalism that had arisen inside the Church. It was a criticism of the clergy by practicing Catholics. One young writer, a teacher in a Jesuit college, had written a novel in which a priest could do nothing for his unfortunate hero. Now, the priest is almost indispensable to the French Canadian novel, as he is to every French Canadian community, and he usually brings comfort or wisdom, sets the recreant on the path to salvation. "But," I asked, "how does the Church take your books?" "Oh, those Catholic squares!" he answered. "Of course they don't like them. They don't understand the Existentialist point of view." So, in spite of what le Frère Untel says, the message of Jean-Paul Sartre has got through to French Canada.

As for le Frère Untel himself, though undoubtedly somewhat anticlerical, he is a loyal and devout Catholic. In the second half of his book—"Frère Untel Ramollit"—he drops his bludgeon and becomes encouraging. In a "Letter to a Young Brother," he warns the neophyte that in the course of his monastic life he must expect to have to contend with laziness, boredom and mediocrity; he must not be too scandalized when he encounters rivalries and jealousies—the struggle for power, in fact. Try not to contribute to this pettiness; make an effort to be open, clear and flexible. Don't allow your conscience to be warped by the Pharisees, who are even more in evidence in the monastery than they are in the outside world. Be prepared to be lonely on occasion—on your birthday, for example, when no one in the monastery will make a fuss about you, or in the case of a not too serious illness, when you will simply be left to yourself. Do not expect results from your teaching. We must always be sowing, but we rarely harvest. As William the Silent said, "One need not hope in order to undertake; nor succeed, in order to persevere." "Humanity needs rocklike men—men appointed once for all. It needs to know that, in the flux of the world, there still exist enduring islets of absolute fidelity and affirmation. The greatest service at the present time that one can render to the human race is to affirm the absolute. The negation of the absolute is the great modern malady. Humanity needs to know that there are men who do not disappear." The pupils of the teaching Brothers must go out and take part in the common life. They will change, they will suffer disillusion. And they will eventually remember their teacher. "What a guarantee of moral support to know that that man is still there, unchanged and un-eroded! All his words, of a sudden, take on value. Ret-roactively, they crystallize in values."

Le Frère Untel and the rebellion of the young are, however, merely local aspects of a larger historical phenomenon: the need of the Catholic Church for such a program of innovation as was initiated by Pope John —who is often invoked by le Frère Untel—in the pro-cedure and practice of the Church and in its attitude toward the non-Catholic world. It has been very im-portant in French Canada that Cardinal Léger of Que-bec should have been one of Pope John's lieuten-ants, who, when the preparations were under way for the Ecumenical Council, spent ten days out of every month in Rome as a member of one of its commit-tees. I do not know how these new policies of the Church have affected other Catholic countries, but I imagine that they have nowhere been more needed or involved in a more serious crisis than they have been in French Canada. Cardinal Léger has encour-aged priests and monks to wear ordinary clerical dress in the streets instead of cassocks or other special robes, and he has presided over the liturgical re-form of the Mass, now delivered from the traditional Latin and made more intimate by responses to the priest on the part of the congregation. "I now have parishes," he boasts, "where a thousand people sing the Mass like angels." He has become a spokesman for the movement for unity among the churches of the Christian world, and he has set up in Montreal—I quote from an article in *Maclean's Magazine* by Mr. Peter Gzowski, to which I am indebted for most of these facts about the situation in Catholic Quebec—"a diocesan committee of priests and laymen, one of the first in the world, to pursue the ecumenical dialogue." Most important of all, Cardinal Léger has set out to reform education by taking it out of the hands of the priesthood. He has, for the first time, appointed non-clerics to the Montreal Catholic School Commission, installed a layman vice-chancellor at the University of Montreal, and handed over to laymen a Montreal college that was formerly directed and staffed exclusively by Catholic priests. He has, says Mr. Gzowski, "pointed proudly to the fact that in some other secondary schools in his archdiocese up to seventy per cent of the teaching hours are now in the hands of the laity." A bill has been recently passed which makes possible the long-needed non-Catholic "neutral school" —that is, a school for French-speaking Protestants, French-speaking Jews and French students from non-believing households. Now, le Frère Untel, in one of the chapters in the second part of his book, presents some constructive proposals which assume that the cause of lay teaching has already been won in Quebec. The lay educators, he believes, must get rid of their hampering bureaucracy and organize a responsible association, like the medical profession or the bar, which understands its own business and protects the interests of the public by preventing the equivalents of malpractice and legal misdemeanor. Besides this, in view of the fact that, at the elementary level of the public schools, the majority of the teachers are women, he believes that these women teachers should give special attention to politics and acquaint themselves with the law, in order to carry weight in determining policies and to become more clearly aware of the implications of these for Canada and the rest of the world.

But the Cardinal and le Frère Untel are up against a powerful conservatism. The Cardinal has some of his bishops against him, and a cardinal cannot dictate to bishops. I heard the guess, when I was recently in Canada, that Léger has twenty-five per cent of the Church on his side and twenty-five against him, with the rest somewhere in between. It has even been reported in the press that he has put in a plea to be transferred to a leper colony in Africa. In view of the fact that Léger has been playing a key role in Canada, I asked why he should want to leave, and was told that he must think it would be easier to deal with African lepers than with the reactionary Canadian clergy, who are fighting "*le laïcisme*." Le Frère Untel himself, after the appearance of his book, disappeared from the Canadian scene, and was said to be working on a thesis in the Catholic town of Fribourg, in Switzerland. In Canada, on one of my visits, I heard two explanations of this: one that he had been removed in order to make him be quiet; the other that he was being groomed to return later on to Quebec and be given an important post in the field of education. On my next visit, two years later, I was told that he was about to return and be given a chair of philosophy in the Catholic University of Montreal, but was then told by someone else that it was still not decided whether or not he should be offered this chair. The contradiction between these reports reflected the situation in French Canada of the two opposing forces in the Church and the uncertainty as to which one would predominate. It is reassuring now to learn that Frère Jérôme (his monastery name) has definitely been given a post in the new Quebec Department of Education which has been authorized by the recent bill.

———————

MAISONS SEIGNEURIALES. Le Frère Untel does not like the Pharisees, and he declares himself strongly a democrat. He tells us that his parents were illiterate. What are the views of the French Canadian aristocrats—that is, of the seignorial families that date from the seventeenth and eighteenth centuries? Representatives of these, too, have been criticizing the barrenness and oppressiveness of the old religious culture, but in a way that is very much less forthright, and, in fact, very nearly inarticulate. I say very nearly inarticulate because, although their recent criticism has made its impression in Canada, they are at first almost incomprehensible to a reader who has no special knowledge of the social group to which they belong. But if this reader persists in exploring the work of such writers as

121

Jean Le Moyne, Anne Hébert and Hector de Saint-Denys-Garneau, he will gradually become acquainted with a psychological atmosphere that seems strangely out of place in the twentieth century in the northern part of North America. These three writers lend themselves readily to being considered together because they constitute a kind of family group. Saint-Denys-Garneau was a first cousin of Anne Hébert's, and Le Moyne was one of his closest friends and one of the editors, after his death, of his work.

The point about all these writers is that they are trying to get away from a milieu which has been stifling them and making them neurotics. This milieu may be identified as the *maison seigneuriale*, the ancestral mansion out of which they have come and which, even when they are no longer living in it, always more or less shadows their writings. This mansion, whether situated in the city or the country, is isolated, dark and damp, and the family who inhabit it, kept static by their stone walls and their Jansenist discipline, are ingrown to the verge of incest, though this is never allowed to take place, or frozen in vindictive hatreds, which are not allowed to come out into the open unless, eventually and abruptly, in acts of violence. This is the kind of household that Hugh MacLennan was doing his best to describe in *Two Solitudes*, but the Protestant Nova Scotian is much too downright and much too purposive to catch the odor of the stale old "*intérieur*" (that rather claustrophobic French substantive), the indeterminate state of mind of souls in the process of asphyxiation. You find it in the writers I have mentioned. Hector de Saint-Denys-Garneau, to whom I shall return later, has a great reputation as a poet, but—except for some pleasant little poems about trees—I myself cannot appreciate his poetry, or the poetry of Anne Hébert. Both tend to run to half-prose strophes that remind me of Paul Claudel—a writer I temperamentally so much dislike that I suppose I cannot do him justice, and so perhaps cannot do them justice, just as I am possibly handicapped by my indifference to William Carlos Williams, in appreciating the current work of the English Canadian poets. This kind of half-prose *vers libre*, from Claudel to Paul Éluard, leaves me cold when it is written in France itself, and the language of the poets mentioned above, with its abstraction and its purified metaphors that do not seem to refer to anything in their actual Canadian world, inflicts on me a mortal chill that seems to freeze my very hand and prevent it from turning the page. Their work is correctly described by Père Baillargeon, in his encyclopedia of French Canadian literature, as both "*hermétique*" and "*poésie dépouillée*."

The fiction of Anne Hébert does take us into the *maisons seigneuriales* and other recognizable Canadian places, but these, too, are rather stripped. And we are partly in a realm of dream. In *Les Chambres de Bois*, much admired by some, a young girl "of the people" is captured and married by the scion of the local mansion, a somewhat sinister place, which "smells of wet ferns and the cedar wardrobe." Young Michel is a dilettante, who paints a little and plays the piano and

123

indulges himself in imaginings of becoming a concert performer. He has a morbid aversion to daylight. In marrying the flattered Catherine, he is trying to secure for himself something "solid and sweet" to nourish his own anemia. But he can only depress and starve her. Leaving his sister in the family *manoir*, he takes his bride to live in the town, in two rooms which he has filled with the family furniture. (The fact that we never know exactly where the story is taking place is characteristic of one kind of French Canadian fiction. The family life described could hardly belong in any country except French Canada, yet Michel and his wife at one point seem to make a trip to southern France. These old-line French Canadians in their cultural enclave on the North American continent do not always quite know where they are.) Though Catherine, when at home, had always been busy with the housework, her husband will not now allow her to do any work at all and insists upon their keeping a servant. They have no visitors, no friends, no children. Poor Catherine does not know what to do with herself. Michel neglects to consummate the marriage till his wife breaks down one day and accuses him of not really loving her. After trying to prove by action that he does, he turns on her as something unclean—*"Tu es le diable, Catherine, tu es le diable!"*—and on one of the rare subsequent occasions when he allows himself to yield to temptation, he complains, after "a brief gleam of pleasure, as if speaking of an evil withdrawing wave, of what a putrid thing love is."

Michel's sister, Lia, very soon moves in on them.

She has been abandoned by a lover who has been living with her in the old house. The young wife feels sorry for Lia. But when Lia makes Catherine read aloud to her, she is cutting about the badness of Catherine's French. She calls her *"petite sotte"* and ridicules Michel for marrying her. Lia takes to painting and makes a mess of the palette with which Michel, in a desultory way, has been doing a portrait of Catherine, and she completely unnerves Michel, who is jealous of her musical competence, by deciding to give a public piano concert. For this purpose she goes away, and Michel, who has done his best to shake her self-confidence, is distraught, nevertheless, by the fear that the concert will be a success, but when he comes to read the newspaper clippings, he is reassured to learn that it has fallen flat. When Lia returns, she declares that she has failed on account of his envy, because he had made her afraid. But she has prepared for him a blow that he cannot avert. In slavish subjection to her lover in the days before he let her down, she has made over to him the family mansion, and now he is going to sell it. Lia and Michel in childhood had made a pact that they would always be faithful to one another, and now, she says, they have both betrayed it, and their very cherished memories of childhood—of the time when their mother was dead and their father had always been out hunting—have been desecrated and lost with the house. The servant has been sent away by Catherine, and she waits upon Michel and Lia, while "glasses, books, cigarettes and ashtrays overflowing with butts were piling up on the carpet—they marked the places

125

where Michel and Lia sat. They hardly moved, and Catherine brought them whitefish and rice twice a day." (Did they really never eat anything else?) Catherine is excluded from their conversations. They play endless games of solitaire.

But now something more plausible happens—I mean more plausible from the outsider's point of view: I am not prepared to say that the story told above is impossible. Catherine has a serious breakdown. She is so ill that she is sent to recuperate at a seaside hotel on some unspecified body of water. And she there meets a handsome young man, of whom it is muttered by her servant that he is "heavy and obstinate, a true peasant." It turns out that he works on a lock. They fall in love, and he asks her to marry him. The reader of French Canadian novels, which usually end in frustration, may expect that Catherine's inhibitions will prevent her from divorcing her husband, but after spending a night with the lusty young man, on what is supposed to be the eve of his departure, she agreeably surprises this reader by telling her lover that she "consents to become his wife." She goes back to the "wooden rooms" where her husband and his sister live. The household is in even worse shape than when she left—"things lost, things dirtied, masterless things"—but now Catherine is able to recognize, as one may "isolate a motif in an abstract and complicated drawing, through the mess of the room, their own kind of order, that sort of encampment on the carpet, at the corner of the fire, that circle of dirty glasses and of ashtrays overflowing with butts, surrounding an open book. 'We were reading,' said Michel to excuse himself. 'It really isn't worth the trouble!' said Lia." She closes the book with a kick and leaves Catherine and Michel alone. He tells her that he has suffered, since she left, "agonies of shame and waiting," but she firmly declares she is leaving, gives Michel back his ring and goes to join her lover. In the literature of French Canada, this ending is unusually cheerful. A vibration from *Lady Chatterley* has perhaps now been felt in Quebec.

For Anne Hébert's masculine opposite numbers, Le Moyne and Saint-Denys-Garneau, the struggle to escape seems more painful. They give somewhat the impression of Michels who are never to succeed in dissociating themselves from the ancient and effete tradition. Hector de Saint-Denys-Garneau, a descendant of an old French Canadian family, already distinguished in literature—François-Xavier Garneau figures as the first important French Canadian historian—was a fragile and ailing young man, culturally starved in Canada, sensitive and reflective and of an extreme scrupulosity of conscience. He died in 1943, at the age of thirty-one. After a visit of three unhappy weeks to Paris, where French Canadians do not feel themselves at home, he had returned to the family mansion at Ste.-Catherine-de-Portneuf, which his parents were still inhabiting, and had gone out to dinner with friends of the family. Later that evening, he paddled a canoe to an island where he was building a camp; but it is assumed—though there was some talk of suicide—that he died of a heart attack, for in the morning his body, nearly frozen, was found among fallen trees.

Hector de Saint-Denys-Garneau is something of a tragic hero for the younger generation in French Canada. There has even been a memorial film of his life, which ends with a shot of the empty canoe. Suicide is a sin for the Catholic Church, and the whispered possibility that the poet may actually have committed this sin seems to have made him appear romantic. Saint-Denys-Garneau's *Poésies Complètes*, which include some posthumous pieces, were published in 1949, and a *Journal* in 1954. The interest of this latter for a non-Canadian is mainly documentary, but in French Canada it is read with reverence and regarded as a significant document. No outburst like le Frère Untel's, it gives expression to the dissatisfactions of a striving and unquiet spirit. It is really—in the French tradition—a collection of moral and aesthetic *"pensées,"* which constitutes a record of Saint-Denys-Garneau's sufferings from Canada's aesthetic poverty. He complains of the general lack of taste, which he says all Canadians recognize. He is dependent for the first-hand enjoyment of painting on the rare exhibitions that come to Montreal, and he writes about Renoir and Cézanne—with a good deal of insight and eloquence— as if he had just discovered them. For music, he is dependent on phonograph records, which he seems always to have to listen to in somebody else's house.

His friend Jean Le Moyne has in this respect been somewhat better off, because at one time he studied the piano and can write about music with some expertise.

But he acknowledges the cultural famine by which they have both been stinted: "It is impossible to estimate the price, in substance, in concentration and in effort that is represented by *Regards et Jeux [dans l'Espace*, the only volume of poems published by Saint-Denys-Garneau] without taking into account the appalling void of the early thirties in Montreal. Today one can incur here heavy debts of humanity, derived from various sources in a society which is relatively rich and diversified, but at that time it was almost inconceivable to owe anything to other people outside a few friends. Speaking strictly, the intellectual and religious milieu of Saint-Denys-Garneau was to consist of four or five intimates. . . . I cannot speak without anger of Saint-Denys-Garneau. For he was murdered. His death was an assassination that had long been prepared beforehand—I do not say premeditated, because we cannot pay that tribute to the consciousness of those who prevented him from living. Who, indeed, were his immediate enemies? Living dead men, victims of themselves, sick men reduced to their wretched fear, but a fear unfortunately endowed with the faculty of communicating itself. One cannot be angry with people who do not know what they are doing, but one can be angry with the state of mind which causes this lack of awareness."

What is Jean Le Moyne railing against? When he tries to explain his resentments, his language is likely to become obscure. It seems to me that both he and Saint-Denys-Garneau write too often in a groping and entangled style—very far from the precision and clarity that one expects from expository French—which resorts to undefined abstractions and unparticularized allusions, and I believe that their opacity is partly due to inhibitions against coming out with what they think, perhaps even to not knowing exactly what they think. The language of the *maison seigneuriale* is as murky as everything else about it, and I blame upon it any clumsiness that may be found here in my translation of certain passages. It is the fear of authority of which everyone speaks that is evidently embarrassing these writers, and the situation reminds one of the case of William Faulkner, who was likely to become blurred and muddled when he was dealing with the unavowed situations created in Mississippi by the mixture of white and black blood. For what these thinkers are trying to emerge from without ever being quite able to get free of it is the dominant influence of the priesthood. They may protest against its Jansenist tyranny, but Jean Le Moyne is very careful to let us know that he makes his submission to the Church, and Saint-Denys-Garneau that he is hoping for grace. In spite of their extreme discomfort, it seems to be impossible for them either to make a clean break with the Church or, like the courageous Teilhard de Chardin, to try to reinterpret Catholicism. When Jean Le Moyne writes about music, he knows exactly what he feels and he can find the words to express it. Nor is he blocked by traditional barriers from following such modern innovators as Hindemith, Stravinsky and Bartók. His descriptions of composers are excellent. But when he writes about the "duality" and "alienation" from which

130

French Canadians suffer, it requires a certain effort on the part of the non-Canadian to understand what he is talking about.

It does not take us long, however, to discover that one of the problems that are worrying the inhabitants of the *maison seigneuriale* is something that in other environments, also, has become one of the main pre-occupations of French Canadian literature: the dichotomy between flesh and spirit that is a feature of Jansenist doctrine. The more advanced thinkers in French Canada have been trying to sew up this dichotomy, but it will obviously be a long time before they can get it to heal. The very terms in which they speak of it betray the malformation of their minds. The recurrence of *"chair,"* *"charnel"* chill the blood of the non-Canadian; they make lovemaking sound so gruesome. It is usually referred to as *"les plaisirs charnels."* There is a novel, for example, by a woman writer with the title *La Chair Décevante,* for *la chair* has always to be conceived as either treacherous or unattractive; *le péché* is always close at hand. We have seen the reactions of Anne Hébert's Michel in the novel described above. In a curious wistful passage in the journal of Saint-Denys-Garneau, when he is longing for a woman's love, we find this horribly worded sentence: *"Or maintenant, me voici avec mon poids de péché originel, sans la possibilité d'un seul repos en la complaisance charnelle."*

Since love has thus been made a sin that must lead to degradation or damnation, it has hardly been found possible in French Canada to write love stories that arrive at fulfillment. *Les Chambres de Bois* is exceptional in that Catherine's love is fulfilled, but her husband, Michel, of course, has never been able to love at all. The persistence of this puritan doctrine in conjunction with certain consequences of a peculiar historical situation has produced a paradoxical attitude. M. Le Moyne on this subject is illuminating. The position of women in French Canada in the early days of colonization was a very important one, which imposed upon them and the men a special kind of relationship. The women were shipped over from France in boatloads, and were almost sure to get married—sometimes at thirteen or fourteen—as soon as they stepped off the boat. It was necessary to populate Canada, and they usually had a child every year. If their husbands, as often happened, were killed by the Indians or the English, they immediately married again. There is a case on record of a woman who married a second husband even before her first had been buried. Through all this, these women were working in their households and the fields and the barns, taking the family through the terrible winters, sometimes fighting the Indians along with their men. These husbands were often away, and the women could never be sure of their coming back. The family unit had become so important that the centrifugal *coureur de bois* and other unmarried men were penalized by being deprived of their hunting and fishing rights, of their freedom to escape to the forest, if they failed to get married within fifteen days after the arrival of a new lot of women, and fathers were even fined if they were slow in marrying off their daughters.

All this, of course, is not unlike the role of the pioneer American woman, who also endured and labored and dominated her ever-expanding family, but the presence of the Roman Catholic Church made the situation in Canada different. Besides these mothers of families, there were the French women missionaries—such as Marie de l'Incarnation—who had immigrated to convert the Indians and who, as mother superiors or directresses of hospitals, came to take on immense responsibilities, sometimes having to withstand siege in their convents, and might eventually occupy positions of very considerable power. They were saints, they were dedicated to the Virgin, and since Mary was a mother as well as a maid, the sacred character of this other aspect was extended to the mothers of families. "The French Canadian mother," says M. Le Moyne, "is something altogether special, for the equivalent of which, I believe, you would look in vain among the civilized people of our time." He depicts her in an apotheosis: "She stands on her linoleum, in calico, in front of a stove and a cooking pot, an infant on her left hip, a large spoon in her right hand, a cluster of little ones about her legs, and a baby in the cradle next to the wood-box." But the paradox is that, with all her fecundity, she is supposed to be inaccessible, since, as mother, like the Virgin, she is sacred. The ordinary husband will refer to his wife as "*la femme*" rather than "*ma femme*," and the strange custom, which the foreign reader dis-

133

covers in French Canadian books, of the lower-class mother and father addressing one another and being addressed by their children as "*sa mère*" and "*son père*" is explained by M. Le Moyne as an example of this dissociation. As a consequence of her mythical role and the behavior that this suggests, it has always been impossible, says M. Le Moyne, to present a genuine woman in French Canadian fiction. "I should be quite unable to discuss, except as a psychologist or a sociologist, the feminine characters who people our fiction and are invoked in our poetry. I cannot find in them a single woman who makes me feel her living presence as does a Princess Casamassima, a Milly Theale, even a Sister Carrie, all American heroines, or any that has the same kind of significance as Mme. Verdurin, as Odette Swann, as Oriane de Guermantes, or as Rachel-quand-du-Seigneur." And there can be no real love affairs. "At the approach of love, whether legitimate or not, or at the idea of an everyday intimacy, something in them [the women in French Canadian novels] is resistant to the consummation, the giving of themselves, or, no matter how passing it may be, to any kind of actual blooming. And the result of this attitude is that the affair does not work out for the men either, who are made to run into obstacles of various kinds, owing to circumstances and to pathology. These gentlemen themselves, besides, are not in very good condition and suffer from various reticences; they readily take a run-out powder [*la poudre d'escampette*], and they do not even shrink from suicide." In these novels, you find "love hindered, love forbidden, love punished, love

134

defiled; anguish in relation to the other party, curbs on self-liberation and on the taking of possession; the futility either of human resources or of having recourse to God; deaths or collapses incurred by them for their having, as lovers, as man and wife, desired to embrace one another, for having wanted *to realize the couple*."

M. Jean-Charles Falardeau and others, in writing about French Canadian fiction, confirm this diagnosis of M. Le Moyne's, and we even find le Frère Untel, in his "Letter to a Young Brother," warning the neophyte not to be timid about remembering that "half the human race is composed of the feminine sex—which of course I hardly need to tell you. It's rather difficult to overlook this fact. Difficult also to overlook the inclination that attracts us toward them. Here or nowhere, he who plays the angel will soon play the beast. So there are women, and these women may be amiable and beautiful. We have promised to live without women. We have had our training far away from them. Too far away, perhaps; I do not mean physically, which is of course obligatory, but intellectually, in the sense that our training in this matter, as in several others, is a little unrealistic." He tells the young Brother that, as long as he is young, he must recognize his hunger for women, that he must reconcile himself to the fact that "any little cutie is more interesting to you than Sainte Marie [Sainte Marie de l'Incarnation]. . . . You will have to endure this hunger, which will go on for a long time, but you mustn't ever be ashamed of it."

This, of course, is a more human attitude, but it is

still a lay brother speaking—that is, one who by a voluntary vow has cut himself off from the other sex.

———————

"Les Demi-Civilisés." The first audacious blow that was struck to let air into this closed French Canadian world was by an unconventional journalist, Jean-Charles Harvey. In March, 1934, Harvey published a novel called *Les Demi-Civilisés*, which caused a scandal and now stands as a landmark. In the perspective of French Canadian literature, in contrast with the obscure discontent of Jean Le Moyne and Saint-Denys-Garneau, this book seems, for its date, quite surprising. It is as if the author had decided to inaugurate, for his blinkered countrymen, a new era of self-consciousness and self-criticism, not with a somber tale of unfilfilment such as those that were to be written by his successors, but by violating with perfect nonchalance every taboo in force in Catholic Canada. His hero describes himself as "a mixture of Norman, Highlander, Marseillais and savage," and Mr. Harvey is himself, I believe, a descendant of one of those Scottish soldiers of Wolfe who became assimilated to the French—which may help to explain his irreverence toward French Canadian institutions.

This irreverence is roundly announced in a kind of prophetic vision that the young hero of the novel is made to have as the result of a traumatic interview with the editor of an important newspaper, to whom he has submitted an article "attempting to show that

136

moral liberty is the pivot of civilization" and who has told him that he will never get anywhere by propounding such "clear and elementary" ideas, that the public only wants "the absurdities that have lived for thousands of years and that will take as many thousands to die." On leaving, the disillusioned young man sinks on to a bench in the park and in a moment finds himself transported to a sterile and unhappy country, where the people are forbidden to think, where such ideas as they are allowed to have are doled out to them in little phials that bear the stamp of the government. On a barren plain, ragged women are pulling up all the roots because there is "an ancient and respectable law" which prohibits growing things. He finds everything plastered with prohibitions, which range from warnings against writing books and attending entertainments which are not a bore to decrees against admiring attractive women and even "being happy in love." (The author allows his hero a great many agreeable love affairs, which are consummated with no scruples on either side.) He finds a woman, "divinely beautiful," hung upside down on a gibbet and whipped by an executioner while the street boys swing on her hair. She is Liberty, and he sets her free, whereupon the earth blooms again. One of the features of that desolate country has been people who are immersed up to their mouths in a filth that is swarming with maggots and flies. They must be forced, the traveller thinks, to assume again their human dignity. No, says Liberty; they, too, must be free, if they prefer it, to live in their excrement.

In the actual world of Quebec, of which this night-mare has been a parable, the hero starts a paper called *The Twentieth Century*, which is liberal though dis-creet and gives a good deal of attention to the arts. This paper has a certain success. But a cynical and clever Parisian becomes a contributor to it and writes an article in which he expresses a doubt as to whether "the good Jesus of the beggars and fishermen" would have any place in a church which has acquired "a monopoly of learning, of the schools and the institu-tions; with its comfort, luxury and opulence built up out of the fishermen's and peasants' tithes." The paper is denounced from the pulpit; subscriptions are can-celled; the office is mobbed. The rich man who has been putting up the money for it tries to persuade the editor to take a less dangerous line and unobtrusively transform it into something conventional, but he pre-fers to let the paper expire. He has attempted to bring to Quebec some news of the culture of the world, and Quebec, when the clergy speaks, has to admit that it cannot accept this. The educated people of French Canada are the "*demi-civilisés*." The peasants are sound enough, but the literate people are still only half baked. They have not yet produced an élite. By a melodramatic plot, the author has separated his hero from the only woman he has ever really loved—a highly intelligent young girl who had procured the money for his paper and enthusiastically followed its progress. In despair, she has condemned herself to en-ter a convent. The hero learns of this the day before she is to take the veil. He tries to get in to see her, and the mother superior shows him the door. But that night the girl has an hallucination that her lover is looking through the window of her cell. She gets up, puts on the gown which is supposed to make her the bride of Christ, jumps out the window and follows the phantom. For two hours she plods through the snow of a heavy and symbolic blizzard and at last falls unconscious, after ringing the bell, in front of her lover's door. He sends for the doctor and revives her by "pouring a few drops of cordial between her lips." But she is raving: "*Ne suis-je pas belle dans ma robe de mariée?*" She confuses the ceremony from which she has fled with offering herself to her lover, and even when her mind clears up, she makes a conscious identification: "*Non, je ne partirai plus. . . . Tu es mon dieu. . . .*" They presumably live happily ever after.

The book—which was only a rather paler version of the kind of thing that H. G. Wells had been writing since the early nineteen-hundreds—brought on Jean-Charles Harvey the same fate that he had invented for the hero of his story. A few weeks after its appearance, the then Cardinal of Quebec (not Léger) denounced *Les Demi-Civilisés* and "under pain of mortal sin, forbade the faithful to read it, to have it about, to lend, buy, sell, print or to circulate it in any way whatever." As a result of this, Harvey was dismissed from the Quebec *Soleil*, for which he had worked fifteen years. He was promised a government job on a condition that was worthy of the Soviet government: that he would publicly repudiate his book and announce that he was withdrawing it from sale. This of course was

139

extremely repugnant, but, as he says in his account of the affair, he had six children and no other means of livelihood, and since the copies of the book in the bookstores belonged not to him but to his publisher, he knew that they would keep on selling. They were, in fact, soon sold out. The Premier promised that Harvey, if he could get some influential priest to approve him, would be given the post of official librarian of the province; but when the matter was referred to the Cardinal, the latter replied to the Premier, "Give him anything except the library." He was assigned to the department of statistics, a subject of which he says he knew nothing. A new Premier, Maurice Duplessis, ordered him to leave Quebec, on account of "having too many enemies." But he was rescued in Montreal by sympathizers who enabled him to found and run "*un journal de combat*" of his own. He is now a respected figure, and *Les Demi-Civilisés* has recently been reprinted, with an introduction in which the author tells its story and points out that "since April, 1934, the lightning has not fallen again upon any of our most daring writers. Have I perhaps been their lightning rod?"

IDYL AND COUNTERIDYL. In 1914, a French novel called *Maria Chapdelaine* became something of a popular success in both the French- and the English-speaking countries. No other book since William Henry Drummond's *The Habitant*, published in 1897, had brought to the outside world any picture of the rural life of the people of French Canada. Yet *Maria Chapdelaine* was not

written by a French Canadian. The author, Louis Hémon, was an adventurous and unconventional Frenchman. Born in Brittany, he studied in Paris for the
French Colonial Service, but decided to be a writer.
He had come to dislike Paris, which he considered
over-refined, and went to England, where he spent
eight years, the products of which were two novels,
Lizzie Blakeston, which dealt with London slum life,
and *Battling Malone*, which dealt with the prize ring.
But he could not accept modern cities, he wanted
something more primitive still, and in pursuit of this
ideal, he came to Canada and hired himself out as a
farmhand at Peribonka in northern Quebec. He was
puzzling to the family he worked for, and they found
him extremely incompetent, but he remained with them
six months. He wrote a novel based on this experience,
but he never lived to see it published: he was killed
by a train in Ontario while walking with a knapsack
on his way to the West.

Maria Chapdelaine is an idyl, which partly accounts
for its popularity, but it is an idyl in a very stern setting. Maria Chapdelaine's father is a professional and
incurable pioneer. He has a mania for clearing land,
and then when the job has been done and a new settlement is under way, instead of staying to enjoy its advantages, he goes on to some other wild region and
starts clearing operations again. This makes life very
difficult for his family. They are always having to
adapt themselves to new inaccesible places, with their
very few friends miles away. In winter, they are often
snowed in, and even at Christmas it is sometimes im-

possible for them to get to the nearest church. Maria Chapdelaine falls in love with a relatively dashing young man from a lumber camp, but when he tries to come to see her in midwinter, he loses his way in the woods, succumbs to the cold and is never seen again. Another young man now presents himself. He has sold his family farm and gone to live in a New England mill town. Maria knows she does not love him, but he tempts her by telling her how infinitely more agreeable life is in the United States: brick buildings, hot water, gas, streetcars, roads that one can walk on without snowshoes. At this point, Maria's mother— one of those monumental Canadian matrons on whom the whole household depends—somehow strains herself and can no longer function. The family cannot believe it: instead of getting on her feet again, she continues to lie groaning in bed. At last they bring a bonesetter and a doctor, over almost impassable roads, from communities many miles away. Neither of them can tell what is wrong. The doctor can only give her sedatives. She dies, and the main responsibility for the household devolves upon Maria. She can hardly now leave her father and her younger brother and sister. She must marry her only other suitor, a young man of no originality, who has nothing to offer her but a life of hard work on a farm as poor and isolated as her father's.

But the author is not content to leave Maria Chapdelaine, as Maupassant would have done, simply the victim of her cruel situation. On the night when she is to make her decision, the spirit of the Province of

Quebec addresses her in a voice "which was half a woman's song and half a priest's sermon. It came like the sound of a bell, like the august peal of church organs, like a naïve complaint and like the piercing prolonged cry of the woodsmen calling to one another in the forest." It tells her that the French had come to Canada three hundred years ago and that everything they had brought with them, "our religion, our language, our virtues, and even our weaknesses, have now become sacred things, unalterable and destined to endure to the end." They are surrounded by aliens whom they call barbarians—who have taken almost all the power and acquired almost all the money—but they know that in the course of the centuries the world will eventually turn to them and say, "These people are of a race that cannot die." And in the meantime they themselves transmit from generation to generation the commandment "In the land of Quebec, nothing is to die and nothing is to change." The point is that Maria Chapdelaine is rejecting, in obedience to this voice, the lure of the life that is offered her by the admirer who has gone to the States. I was reminded by this end of the story of the very similar ending of *Colette Baudoche*, a novel by Maurice Barrès, which came out a few years before *Maria Chapdelaine*. In this book, a young girl of Metz, thirty-eight years after the defeat of the French, is on the point of marrying a Prussian professor when attendance at a Mass for the soldiers who were killed in 1870 revives in her the patriotism of Alsace-Lorraine and prevents her from going through with it. Here it is the author himself who

143

apostrophizes his heroine, but in much the same vein as the Province of Quebec in *Maria Chapdelaine*. The political motivation in Louis Hémon's novel strikes for me the same false note. I find it rather hard to believe that a young peasant girl in this kind of dilemma would be influenced by ancestral voices that address her in editorial rhetoric. I imagine that Hémon was echoing Barrès, though it appears that there is a native precedent for the attitude of Maria Chapdelaine. In one of the first French Canadian novels of any note, *Les Anciens Canadiens*, by Philippe Aubert de Gaspé (published in 1863), a young Scotchman falls in love with the sister of a French former schoolmate, but in the course of the war with the English, he is forced, at the orders of Wolfe, to burn down the French family's *manoir*. The girl refuses to marry him. This is much like our novels of the Civil War, in which the lovers are separated or inhibited by belonging to opposite sides. Such conflicts, of course, may arise, but I feel that Maria's revelation has been dragged in by the need of the author to give a more or less rational explanation for the persistence of the French Canadians in sticking so doggedly to their poverty and ignorance.

Maria Chapdelaine is now quite out of fashion. The voice of Quebec is no longer so patient but has become, as I shall later show, extremely belligerent and bitter. Yet the book was an important event in the literature of French Canada. To have had their own life described by a Frenchman who had brought to it an eye both artistic and sociological made the native writers more aware of the peculiar features of that life and of its literary possibilities. The result, says Père Baillargeon, was that *Maria Chapdelaine* furnished a formula for a whole series of peasant idyls (though I note that M. Gilles Marcotte contends that the native fiction was already taking this direction). The present writer has been deterred from much research into this aspect of French Canadian fiction—as well as of its English Canadian counterpart—by a very strong disinclination to read novels of rural life that take families of simple people through the years and the generations. In these books, the changes of the seasons are always described at length; the crops are planted and harvested, and sometimes the crops fail, and this makes things even more depressing; the animals give birth to their young, and they have to be herded and fed; there are love affairs that develop very slowly; the young people grow gradually old, and the old people pass away; everybody is dedicated and tied to the land. The only agricultural novel that I remember to have thoroughly enjoyed is Zola's once scandalous *La Terre*, in which primitive country life is made so outrageously horrible that it finally becomes comic.*

* I have learned for the first time, since the above was written —from Gérard Tougas's *Histoire de la Littérature Canadienne-Française*—that French Canada has had a kind of Zola in Albert Laberge (1871-1960). His novel, *La Scouine*, says Mr. Tougas, is to French Canadian literature what *La Terre* is to French. It took Laberge fifteen years to write and was only published in 1918—at the author's own expense, as were all his other books—in an edition of sixty copies. In this and other fictions in the same vein, Laberge, "with firm stride and quick eye, went all over Chateauguay, his flowery little corner of earth, to distil the most lugubrious prose of Canadian literature. The more he is inundated with joy at his contact with the tutelary

145

I have not read *Trente Arpents*, by Ringuet or *Le Survenant*, by Germaine Guèvremont, but I have found one French Canadian idyl that is distinguished and quite delightful. *La Petite Poule d'Eau*, by Gabrielle Roy, deals with the family of a sheep farmer—even more remote and isolated than the family of Maria Chapdelaine—who are the sole inhabitants of an island in northern Manitoba. Since the only school is eighteen miles off, over an almost untraversable road, the government is obliged to provide a special teacher for the seven children, who is condemned to go and live with them on the island—first, a Frenchwoman, whom the children adore and who stimulates an ambition to learn, then a British one, who does not know how to get on with the French and who discourages them by lectures on Dominion patriotism that they do not understand. The family is visited at long intervals by a polyglot Belgian priest, who mixes saintliness with a good deal of shrewdness. We follow him on his adventures as he goes about his ministrations among the French and the Scottish, the Poles and the Ukrainians, the Finns and the Swedes and the Icelanders, and ends with a festive gathering—almost an apotheosis—in celebration of one

---

trees and the heady perfume of the flowers, the more gloomy does his written thought become. Has he not arrived, in old age, at a sort of masochistic coquetry? . . . If his story seems to be carrying him away from a dramatic and painful end, a pitiless nemesis will bring it about that this woman in whom we are beginning to be interested gets suddenly burned alive in an unforeseeable fire or that that solid peasant falls down dead in the road, preferably with his nose sticking into a pad of cow dung, which has been freshly deposited at that spot by the attentive care of the novelist."

146

of his visits: a banquet, a little sermon; the young people dance. There in the Northwest, so thinly populated, the different national strains are able to mingle on jovial terms. The caller for the square dance is a Scot, but he presently begins calling in French. He thinks with affection of "*ce beau pays*," France. The priest lights up his pipe. "Above his head shone millions of bright stars. The lightning bugs in the grass gave out little sparkles of light." To the priest, too, "the old civilization seemed far away, gracious and kind. The farther he had gone toward the North, the freer he had been to love."

Louis Hémon makes his French Canadian peasants the servitors of an austere ideal; Gabrielle Roy invests hers with a kind of sentimental jollity that reminds one of the many American books about humble people of various nationalities in the period—the early nineteen-hundreds—when *Mrs. Wiggs of the Cabbage Patch* was popular. These idyls of country life were to give way to a kind of anti-idyl. One of the features of this anti-idyl was that it abandoned the country for the city; but before I go on to deal with the French Canadian novels of urban life, I want to speak of a writer in a class by herself—Mlle. Marie-Claire Blais, who has so far shown herself incapable of allowing life in French Canada to appear in a genial light or to seem to embody any sort of ideal.

Not that Mlle Blais is a realist. Her novels—and this, as I have said, is quite common in Canadian fiction—are not even localized in Canada. The only one that is given a definite setting is supposed to take place in France. Yet these stories could hardly have emanated from any other country than French Canada. Mlle Blais is a true "phenomenon"; she may possibly be a genius. At the age of twenty-four, she has produced four remarkable books of a passionate and poetic force that, as far as my reading goes, is not otherwise to be found in French Canadian fiction. Her countrymen, in reviewing these books—since the astonished acclamation provoked by the first—have not been particularly kind to her; but I have been glad to find my opinion confirmed in an article by another young French Canadian woman writer, Mlle Suzanne Paradis, who, with a generosity rare among literary competitors, announces that of all the new novelists Mlle Blais alone is unmistakably recognizable as the real thing. The first of her books, *La Belle Bête*, written when she was eighteen and published in 1959, is a story of country life that is in its narrower way as shocking as Zola's. It is another tale of isolation: a widow and her two children on a farm. The daughter, who is ugly, hates her younger brother because, although an idiot, he is extremely good-looking—"*la belle bête*." She also hates her mother, who, vain of her own charms, dislikes the daughter and spoils the idiot. The mother takes a lover, a broken-down dandy, who comes to live with the family and whom both the children loathe. The idiot manages to kill him by riding him down on horseback. In the meantime, the daughter has married a blind man, who cannot see how ugly she is and imagines her to be very beautiful. When he suddenly regains his sight and sees that he has been cheated, he leaves her. She now has a little daughter, whom she believes to be as ugly as herself. She returns with the child to her mother's. The idiot is sent to an asylum. The mother is afflicted with cancer of the cheek, which she tries to conceal with makeup. The daughter becomes sickened with the situation and throws a lighted lamp into a haycock. When the idiot, escaped from the asylum, makes his way back to the farm, he finds everybody and everything in ashes. He goes off to take a drink from the lake and sees in the water that he has lost his beauty. He throws himself in and drowns.

The second book, *Tête Blanche*, deals with people on a somewhat higher social level. It is the story, mostly told in letters, of a bitter intelligent boy, cruelly neglected by his actress mother and cruelly separated from the girl he loves. These novels of Marie-Claire Blais are the most unrelievedly painful that I remember ever to have read, and one questions, as in Thomas Hardy, the inevitability of so much pain. One asks why, for example, it is necessary that Tête Blanche should lose his Émilie, who has given him every sign of reciprocating his love. Their separation is fortuitous and need not be permanent. If he had had a little more gumption, we think, he would have looked her up again—unless we are to suppose that his mother's neglect has made him pessimistic about women. (Translations of both these novels have been published by Little, Brown, the first as *Mad Shadows*, the second with the French title.)

Tête Blanche takes place in a recognizable world—school days, college, holidays at the seaside—but the next novel, *Le Jour est Noir*, passes like a troubled dream. It reminds one—though I find it more moving —of the shadow world of Anne Hébert. *La Belle Bête*, in subject and tone, may perhaps have some relation to the story of Anne Hébert's called *Le Torrent*, in which a boy provokes a stallion to trample his hated mother to death, and the characters and happenings of *Le Jour est Noir* are even more floating and unreal than those of *Les Chambres de Bois*. We find that we are sometimes following a narrative, sometimes, and without warning, listening to unspoken soliloquies going on in the characters' minds. Though Marie-Claire Blais herself does not come out of the *manoir seigneurial*, she has caught over something of its mood. She heads one of the sections of *Le Jour est Noir* with a characteristic quotation from a poem of Anne Hébert's: "Retrace your steps, O My Life, you can see that the street is closed." Death and suffering dominate this novel, which is really less a novel than a poem in prose, like a story by Walter de la Mare. It made me think of de la Mare's *The Riddle*, in which the seven children one after another go up to the mysterious oak chest in the room where they have been told not to play, get into it and are not ever seen again. The people in *Le Jour est Noir* cannot sustain any intimate relationship. Wives and husbands abandon one another; mothers abandon their children. In Mlle Blais's two preceding books, the principal theme is the anguish of children to whom love has been denied by their mothers, but here we are evidently to sympathize with the mother who will not love her children. The characters

Marie-Claire Blais. *Portrait by Mary Meigs*

expire or drift away; sometimes they return, after years. A married man, for some obscure reason—a guilt that the reader cannot grasp—after telling his wife that he will be back for dinner, that he is going for a walk in the winter woods, turns out to have hanged himself. Everybody talks about dying. "Yance, we are summoned to die, in this family we love death. That is our misfortune." . . . "I hear the words of Raphaël [the husband of Yance], when I announced to him that I was expecting a child: 'What an idea, Yance, to bring a child into the world! Are you sure, then, of this world?' . . . The child next to my heart, the interrogation of Raphaël, confronted by the future and the present, becomes mine, too. I am no longer on terms of confidence with the generation that my daughter carries under her innocent brow. A night with no waking is shadowed before me: are we condemned to die? Are we the dark generation, chosen to look on at the end of the universe? Is this doubt but a presentiment of a horrible fatality? Is Raphaël cynical from fear? Is Josué weak for the same reason? Is he suffering from an absurd panic in face of his own death? His poor little death? It is true that the beings of our generation have to suffer from advancing into an age of destruction. They deliberately choose abysses on the scale of their dreams." . . . "I am nursing my baby, Josué [another couple is here involved]; you have turned away your head because you know that this moment is the most intimate for me: you sit at my knees and do not move. Your life, my life are torn from us drop by drop by a little child's body." Mlle.

151

Blais tends always toward images of desolation. "When you are the child of the waters and the beaches, you feel yourself called by the wind. I lived on my island till I was thirteen years old. Then the cities were opened before me like wounds." . . . "I shall see them [the snows of my country] again. The snows have taken root in me. You don't understand, Marie-Christine. The snows become an excuse for the laziness of body and mind. You belong to a journey. I am the man of a country in which nature is as solitary as man."

The next published work of Mlle Blais, *Les Voyageurs Sacrés* (in the collection Écrits du Canada Français), is even more a prose poem than *Le Jour est Noir* and is in fact given the subtitle *Poème*. The scene here is laid in France, and the story is a traditional French triangle—husband and lover and wife—presented, however, in a form which is almost as symphonic and unconventional as that of *L'Année Dernière à Marienbad*. The married couple have established for themselves a perfect pattern of "gracious living," based presumably on a personal harmony of tenderness, sensibility and taste; but this union is to be upset by the sudden impingement on their lives of a brilliant Viennese pianist, who has come to play Mozart in Paris. At first the couple share their admiration for him, as they have been sharing everything else; then a play by the husband is a failure. The pianist lays siege to the wife. The something wrong, the something wanting that has always been wanting, in the relations of husband and wife is uncomfortably and subtly conveyed as they try to go on serenely with their systematic visits to cathedral towns. The wife yields at last to the pianist. The husband throws himself into the Seine. The wife says farewell to her lover and follows her old companion in death. The pianist, however, is delighted by the news that his wife in Vienna has just had another baby. But it is almost as inappropriate to attempt to summarize in this way a work as lyric as *Les Voyageurs Sacrés* as it would be *The Waves* of Virginia Woolf.

In reading the most recent works of Mlle Blais, one sometimes becomes a little annoyed by the solemn and portentous dialogue and a constant repetition of surnames that reminds one of Maeterlinck; and yet she has developed so fast—each of her books has been different from the one before—that she will no doubt soon have outgrown this, and these works, like her volumes of poems, *Pays Voilés* and *Existences*—though the second of these is somewhat haunted by the to me insufferable presence of Paul Claudel—contain bold and beautiful images of a kind that had hardly appeared in the rather bleak *La Belle Bête*. What all of her works, however, do more or less have in common are the familiar Canadian themes of the fugitive or exile from society and the dislocated love affair. The figure of the priest is not present, and we hear nothing of the official cult; but Mlle. Blais has grown up in this cult, and the idea that man is born to sorrow, the agony of expiation, is at the base of her tragic consciousness. Yet her work has more than local interest. It is the refinement to a purer kind of poetry than that of the protesting patriots of the desperate cry that arises from the poverty, intellectual and material, the passionate self-punishing piety and the fierce defeated pride of Quebec.

Mlle Blais was educated in a convent in Quebec, where she spent eleven years and managed to read not only such classical French literature as was approved by the convent authorities but also the anarchic writers, from Rimbaud to the Surréalistes, who would undoubtedly have filled them with horror. I was astonished, when I inquired of Mlle Blais by what authors she felt she had been influenced, to have her answer Lautréaumont's *Les Chants de Maldoror*, Cocteau's *Thomas l'Imposteur*, and André Breton's *Nadja* —which I never should have suspected from her work and of which I could see no clear traces. She afterwards added Claudel and Mauriac, which seemed to me more comprehensible.

When she had written *La Belle Bête*, she gave the manuscript to Père Georges-Henri Lévesque, the remarkable Dominican monk who has played such an important role in the cultural life of Quebec. Père Lévesque had been the founder and the head of the School of Social Sciences at Laval University, and he had had a good deal to do with the awarding of literary prizes and scholarships. His attempts to modernize education had aroused against him the conservative old guard of the clergy and the dictator-Premier Duplessis, and it was perhaps under pressure from them that the authorities of the University set a limit to the tenure of the heads of departments, so that Lévesque was obliged to withdraw. At this time, in 1955, he established at Montmorency, just outside Quebec, a unique institution of culture. La Maison Montmorency had been the residence of an eighteenth-century English governor and the *pied-à-terre* of the Prince of Wales when Queen Victoria sent him to Canada to sober him up. It has now been converted by Père Lévesque into a kind of combination of the Peterborough Colony and the New School for Social Research. Here Catholics can make their retreats, but scientists and artists also can find a refuge in which to work. The house is also available to serious organizations, Protestant as well as Catholic, for the purpose of holding meetings or conferences. Between September, 1955, and September, 1959, there were hundreds of clerical gatherings, reunions of the Federation of Classical Colleges, sessions of "*syndicats ouvriers, agricoles et coöpératifs*," cultural and social meetings, and conferences on international, national, provincial and regional affairs. An illustrated booklet on La Maison Montmorency describes its purpose as follows: "Being convinced that everything which contributes to the liberation of man from his prejudices, his pettiness, and his anxieties may throw open the way to Christ, [the directors] have believed that the discreet presence—on the hill of Montmorency—of monks whose profession it is to clear away the shadows and to live in peace would be for our generation, so hungry for the freedom of truth, a hope and an invitation." In a pamphlet called *Le Chevauchement des Cultures*, which contains an address delivered at a conference of the Canadian Institute of Public Affairs, we find Lévesque, whose

English is excellent, recommending an uninhibited interchange between the French and the English cultures. Culture, he says, must be open and universal; it must be free to enrich itself from any source. "A culture which pretended to be *human, French, and Catholic* but which sought to remain closed would be simply a triple contradiction in terms." When Père Lévesque read Marie-Claire Blais's manuscript, he arranged to have it published and secured for her a travelling scholarship that would give her a year in France. When people asked how he, a Dominican monk, could bring himself to sponsor a book filled with such horrors and a book in which religion was never invoked, he would reply that real talent was so precious and so rare that when one found it one could only encourage it.

Mlle Blais, after leaving the convent, took courses in literature and philosophy at Laval University, in her native city of Quebec. She has studied English and German and is a voracious reader in English as well as in French. In 1963, she was awarded a Guggenheim Fellowship, and she is now living in the United States. If one already knows her books, it is rather surprising to meet her. She has almost the appearance of a schoolgirl, with fine little features and hands and feet, and when I took her out to dinner in Boston, I found that I usually had difficulty in getting the waiters to serve her with drinks, because they could not believe that she was not under age, and she finally had to take the precaution of bringing her passport along. She does not strike one, however, as callow, and a very first-rate mind is seen in her avidity for intellectual experience and in the intensity of her personal responses to everything she sees or reads.

———

THE REALISTS. The first serious large-scale attempts on the part of French Canadian novelists to deal with the life of the urban lower classes were made during the last war, when Roger Lemelin, in 1944, published *Au Pied de la Pente Douce* and Gabrielle Roy, in the following year, published *Bonheur d'Occasion*. These books at the time made a considerable impression and are still regarded as important events, but here again the non-Canadian reader must recognize that the interest of a book in the context of a local situation may not necessarily coincide with its interest as literature seen in a larger context. Such a reader will have some difficulty in getting through these long prosaic novels. They are what used to be called "realistic," and follow a method that one already knows well from many novels that have presented the more lusterless aspects of other Western urban societies, in which modern industrialization came earlier and is further advanced than it has been in the Province of Quebec.

Mme Roy's *Bonheur d'Occasion* is a much more ambitious book than *La Petite Poule d'Eau*, yet its ambitious intention turns out, from the point of view of literary art, to be rather a handicap. *Bonheur d'Occasion* is serious, well observed, very competently written, though it has none of the charm or humor of *La*

Petite Poule d'Eau (published in 1951). It takes us back to the age of George Moore and Arnold Bennett, when the French naturalism of the nineteenth century had belatedly reached the English-speaking countries. Like Bennett, when he wrote about the Staffordshire Five Towns, Mme Roy, in writing about Montreal, builds a solid mass of drab streets and buildings, weaves a texture of homely happenings and commonplace conversations. It takes her almost three pages to tell of a short journey by streetcar and bus, one page of which is occupied with a detailed account of a girl getting her lipstick out of her bag and noticing a run in her stocking. A young man walking from his lodging to a rendezvous at a cinema is described at a length of ten pages, which involves exact specifications as to all the streets through which he passes, and careful accounts of the river boats, the railroad, the grain elevators and the telegraph wires—with all of which this young man must have been so familiar that at such a time he would scarcely have noticed them and which only discourage such interest as the author has been able to create in regard to the results of the rendezvous, which, as it turns out, is not to take place. We have none of the sensations of drama that Hugh MacLennan is able to impart to the material, almost equally graceless, provided by the city of Halifax.

Au Pied de la Pente Douce is equally hard going, but it is Lemelin's first book, written when he was twenty-five, and the difficulty of reading it is perhaps largely due to a difficulty on the part of the author in getting hold of and finding out how to manipulate his

158

then unexploited material—the sordid, swarming and sometimes repellent life at the bottom of the Rock of Quebec. We are here, in the Quartier Saint-Sauveur, in what is called the Basse-Ville, far below the parks and the museums, the churches and the convents of the august old town. To the people who live below, the great hotel, the Château Frontenac, built by the Canadian Pacific Railway, is a place for Americans on vacation, which these natives hardly dare to invade. Here we find the same dogged illiteracy, the same primitive superstition and the same incomprehension of hygiene that we do in the rural novels. Here, as in *Bonheur d'Occasion*, the fathers, no longer tied down to the demanding routine of the land, become idle, drunken and boastful; the mothers can no longer control a flock of children turned loose on the city. In this novel and in its two successors, as in *Two Solitudes* and *Bonheur d'Occasion*, the political and religious problems that agitated French Canadians at the time of the Second World War are given a good deal of attention, and they are treated by Lemelin in the tone of uniform irony that was established in French fiction by Flaubert. In *Au Pied de la Pente Douce* he is attempting to present a "cross-section" of the life of a social organism, and as a story it is rather chaotic. The real center of interest is a boy in his late teens called Denis Boucher, who is brilliant, independent and rebellious. He has started with the great advantage of having parents who can read and write, and he obtains tangible evidence of his talent by winning a prize in a fiction contest. He imagines himself constantly in noble roles

159

and treats his neighbors with a certain condescension; his relations with his family, his closest friend and the girl he sometimes thinks he loves are shifting and indeterminate. No clear situation emerges, and we are given, at the end of the story, no hint of what direction his life is to take.

When, however, we read Lemelin's two subsequent novels, *Les Plouffe* and *Pierre le Magnifique*, we discover that the three volumes constitute a kind of trilogy, all hung upon, though not entirely centered about, the career of Denis Boucher. The Plouffes of the second of these books are a family of the Basse-Ville—the father is employed as a printer—who are evidently intended to be typical of the aspiring lower middle class. But the novel tends to revolve around Denis Boucher, who, now twenty, becomes a reporter and, as an enthusiastic nationalist, gets both the old Plouffe and himself fired from the paper they have been working for, the conservative *Action Chrétienne*, when he writes for a nationalist journal a sharply anti-British story that calls attention to the hostile behavior of the Plouffes on the occasion of the visit of the King and Queen. The father had failed to put out a flag, and one of the sons had pitched a baseball past "the nose" of the royal car. When the Second World War begins and Denis discovers that the Bishop of Quebec is all for the Allied cause and will abstain altogether from the fight that the clergy have been putting up against the Ottawa federal government, he becomes discouraged with nationalism and goes to Europe as a war correspondent. In the third of these related volumes, we find Denis, now thirty, living quietly in Quebec with a mistress and leading a more or less bohemian life. He does not seem to have come to anything, and his relations with his mistress are unstable. He asserts that his failure to succeed is due to his "having been born with this instinct of revolt against society and all its pettiness. . . . Life is too short for me to sacrifice my taste for the infinite to a few years of ambition and success."

Denis's equilibrium, such as it is, is suddenly upset by the appearance of another rebellious younger boy, whom he comes to identify with his younger self. Pierre Boisjoly, like Denis, has emerged from a background of poverty. He is being put through a seminary by a benevolent and innocent old priest; but he eventually decides that this has been a mistake, that he does not really have the vocation, and he breaks the heart of his patron when he refuses, after finishing with honors at the preparatory Petit Séminaire, to go on to the Grand Séminaire. Now Denis guiltily feels that the effect on Pierre of his getting to know himself and his mistress has had some influence on the boy's decision, and, in compunction, he wants to do something to help him to go on with his education. Pierre's mother works as a charwoman for a well-to-do Quebec family, whose son, an obnoxious and stupid boy, has been one of Pierre's schoolmates, and the son and the mother both are resentful of Pierre's achievements. They revenge themselves by treating the boy with all the insulting superciliousness of which Quebec upper-class-consciousness is capable. Pierre's mother has discovered accidentally a cache of money in her employer's house, and Denis—reverting to the lawlessness of his boyhood, when we first met him in *Au Pied de la Pente Douce*, as a member of a neighborhood gang—decides to break in and steal the money in order to make it possible for Pierre to finish his education. Pierre gets wind of this and tries to prevent it, and the robbery results in a fiasco, which involves the accidental death of the grandmother of the spiteful schoolmate. More feelings of guilt for Pierre, who is already feeling guilty at having let down the old curé.

The story of Denis and Pierre is now to take a turn that, for the reader not accustomed to French Canadian fiction, is likely to be unexpected. Though Pierre is a Catholic renegade and Denis by now a cynic, they both have a terror of women, the instinct to shrink from "*la chair.*" Denis Boucher in his youth has regarded it as a sign of weakness to fall in love with a woman, but he has been tempted by a physical appetite for a convent-bred *jeune fille* who is mad about him. He treats her brutally and lets her go. The most sensitive of the Plouffe brothers, Ovide, has been bitterly humiliated when a girl he has hoped to woo and to induce to share his great passion, opera, is stolen by his athlete brother. He decides to enter a monastic order and spends a year of preparation in a monastery, but he emerges from this at once when he is given a hint by Denis that the girl is still interested in him. He takes her to the Château Frontenac, where she introduces him to Singapore Sling cocktails. In a taxi, she kisses his neck: "*Ovide . . . s'donnait à des calculs méticuleux . . . sur les possibilités de cueillir une parcelle de plaisir charnel.*" He takes her to a quiet spot by the wall of a monastery, where she offers herself with abandon, but the cocktails are wearing off, and the monks inside the monastery strike up a midnight chant. "*Habillez-vous, petit démon!*" he yelps. She bursts into tears and flees. (One gets to feel very sorry for these women in French Canadian novels.) Ovide rushes to a priest, but the priest is absorbed in a book and receives him with complete indifference, telling him to come round the next day. Now, Pierre has been strongly attracted by Denis Boucher's mistress, Fernande, whom Denis, with characteristic abruptness, has abandoned after the night of the robbery. She has also been much drawn to Pierre, but they have lost sight of one another and she has married a swinish husband. When they meet again, there seems to be no reason that they should not attain their desire, and the non-Canadian reader is awaiting the consummation. The lovers are alone in Pierre's room, and the scene seems to be all set. Unreservedly they declare their love; they are "made for one another." But to yield to it would mean adultery, and, besides, Pierre has had in the meantime a particularly disgusting glimpse of a drunken debauch with prostitutes. "Go to bed here and wait for me," he says. He wants to think over the situation. "If I should stay now, we should both be vanquished, and you would share in a punishment that is deserved by me alone." He goes to see Denis Boucher and denounces him for having corrupted and ruined both Fernande and himself. Denis learns that Fernande is with Pierre, and the interview at once arouses in him feelings of jealousy as well as of guilt. He dashes off to confess to a priest, who turns out to be the good old man who put Pierre through the seminary. Pierre returns to Fernande and tells her that *"tout est fini."* Denis bursts in with the priest. Pierre says farewell to Fernande and goes away with the priest to confess. He now knows that he does have the vocation and that he will enter the Grand Séminaire.

Among the best features of Lemelin's novels are the portraits of clerical characters. When the first of his books appeared, he was scolded for bad taste and irreverence, but in his handling of the clergy there is at least as much respect as satire. It may be interesting in this connection to quote from an article of Lemelin's in a paper called *Le Collectioneur*, written in answer to the question "Are you an agnostic?" In his childhood, Lemelin says, "I was up to my neck in the Catholic religion, as other people are Negroes. My advice had never been asked, nor do I ask my children for theirs." Later on, reading Renan and other authors, "I became almost completely detached from the Faith." He tried to reject Church and family. "A deep need for irreverence incited me against everything that seemed to me most sacred." He "rebelled against the temporal face of the Church and in certain of its representatives could see nothing except ignorance and absurdity." But "just as the rebellious bad boy does not, on that account, deny the existence and the enormous presence of his father, so my little run-ins with the clergy have not for an instant made me doubt that

164

God was the force behind everything, or the divine character of the Church of Christ." His health has been so good and he has been kept so busy, he says, that he has never known "those spiritual crises which one hears so much about in novels." He did not cease to be a practicing Catholic, but his observances became perfunctory. It was later that, "in the perspective of intellectual curiosity, I turned more seriously toward my religion," and he decided that since he was an artist and since "nothing exalts me more than the phenomenon of transposition, which, by a sort of inexplicable miracle makes it possible for man to multiply himself infinitely in beauty," he must accept the revelation of the Church. "Every transposition in the realm of art brings us close to God. What a grandiose, what an incomparable transposition, coming from God, in the inverse sense, is His incarnation in Christ, and multiplying itself, through His death, over the centuries in in ourselves. . . . I am happy to belong to a religion all of whose principles rest on love and charity. By its temporal role in society, I have recognized that the Church was my principal ally in the education of my children and that it is through her that, in this so terribly dangerous age, I can be most sure of making men of them. I try to bring to the priesthood an understanding which I was incapable of giving them in my youth. When they have weaknesses, my first impulse is to help them; they are no longer authority but my brothers. For our clergy forms an intimate part of the French Canadian family."

It seems difficult to live in French Canada and not in some way come to terms with the clergy.

Lemelin has improved as a writer. His first book was confused and elliptical; he was clumsy in handling his characters; it has to be plodded through. *Pierre le Magnifique*, on the other hand, has a straight unencumbered story line, and is amusing and exciting throughout. And yet M. Lemelin says that he will write no more books of this kind. The Plouffes were transferred to television in a soap opera that departed from the novel in being much more sentimental and humorous. The series was done both in French and in English by the same cast of actors, and it ran, I am told, for years. The Plouffes have now become a cliché for the lovable French Canadian family—Denis Boucher was very soon dropped—and are as much of a bore to the intelligent young as Maria Chapdelaine. But M. Lemelin has announced that his imaginative work in the future will be aimed at the wider audience. One can quite understand that it must be disheartening to write for the small group of readers that literate French Canada provides. M. Lemelin now owns a small sausage factory and likes to speak of himself as a businessman. He has become, in Quebec City, a well-known and well-liked figure, though he is looked at a little askance by professional literary people, who do not approve of his failure to follow up his early career. He has something of the jauntiness and perversity of his recurrent Denis Boucher, and, as in the case of his complicated hero, one cannot be sure whither he is headed.

M. Lemelin, when I was in Quebec City, took me to lunch at the Garrison Club, which was founded after what the French call "the Conquest" and is one of the oldest clubs in North America. The membership was originally confined to resident English Canadian officers—old colonels, said Lemelin, who had been on safaris. But the French have now been admitted, and they constitute, in fact, today, the majority of the membership. The French Canadians say that the club is much gayer than it was, and that the English themselves enjoy it more. In those ample and comfortable rooms, which are still rather plain, bleak and British, and as one passes through the gallery of photographs, in the corridor that leads to the dining room, of square-shouldered and mustachioed English officers, encased in their uniforms, one feels that this may well be the case.

I have sometimes been retelling the incidents of novels that are interesting as documents on the special conditions of French Canada but that are not, as I have said above, necessarily to be recommended to the general reader of fiction. In the case of André Langevin, however, the general reader may simply be sent to his books—especially *Poussière sur la Ville* (1955) and *Le Temps des Hommes* (1956), which seem to me to stand very high in the fiction of his generation. These somber stories have a moral interest, as well as a tragic force, that make them parables of human destiny and not merely reports on the local life. They are also extremely well told. The stagnancy of life in French Canada has in the past been reflected in many of its novels by a certain paralytic quality. It has been rather unusual for them to proceed along a well-paced course and arrive at a determined end; their progress is likely to be sluggish, as if blocked by heavy impediments, and they sometimes go round in loops. They are as different as possible in this respect from our own American novels, which are likely to carry us along even when they are not going anywhere. It is true that Langevin's first novel, *Évadé de la Nuit* (1951), has many of the forbidding features of French Canadian fiction. It is turbid and moves rather sullenly, and it is deadened by a doom of frustration that does not seem to be wholly warranted by the handicaps of the orphaned hero. The lugubrious and leaden vocabulary that sometimes makes these novels so oppressive is never allowed to lift: *"l'angoisse," "la douleur," "la souffrance," "la misère,"* and, always lurking in the background, *"la mort."* But the same author, in the novels that follow, has managed to get free of all this. He never stumbles; he makes rapid progress; as a narrator, he goes into action. Nor does he diminish the importance of his characters by rearing around them vast walls of naturalistic detail, though his godforsaken little industrial towns and his desolating winter forests are made as real to us as if we had been there. His books belong to the class of which it is said that you cannot put them down, and they leave a lasting impression.

These novels also make connections with that international school of thought of which le Frère Untel complained that the Catholic universities knew nothing: the Existentialism of Jean-Paul Sartre. The conception of the moral obligation to persist in a chosen course of conduct from which no definite results can be hoped, in a world that makes no sense in relation to it, was originally inspired, I believe, by the predicament of Frenchmen like Sartre at the time of the German occupation, when they continued, discouraged but obstinate, to carry on with the French Resistance. The situation of intelligent young Catholics in Canada must sometimes seem equally discouraging. John Buell's second novel, *Four Days*, is evidently an extreme example of what the Existentialists call "the absurd." The boy must persist, without hope, in a course that is, without his really grasping it, not merely anti-social but quite senseless. In Langevin, the principal characters stick to courses that are apparently futile and have a moral value only for the men themselves. This theme is first stated very clearly in *Évadé de la Nuit*: "That which, an hour before, could have still been called a jeu d'esprit was becoming a decisive ordeal. To gamble everything on the chance of winning everything, but with lucidity, in an orderly manner. To recreate another's soul, without love, without pity, especially. And, for stakes, one's own resolution in a world that was indecipherable." And later, when the wife is in labor: "The suffering body on the bed was doing his life violence, was giving it a direction, obliterating the past. The chains which were being forged could not be easily broken. It would be happiness or nothing, nothingness. Finished was the blind advance

169

into a hostile universe: a cell was forming itself of which he would be the nucleus, the nourisher. He no longer belonged to himself. Why should he exert himself to find a meaning now? He had already committed himself, and the road which he had come was closing behind him, was being effaced in a sea of sand, which did not preserve even his footprints. And, for the first time, he saw his way, stretching straight ahead, even to death." His wife dies; the baby survives, but he abandons it as he has been abandoned when he was sent by his own father to an orphan asylum. He plunges into the winter forest and sinks into the deep snow. He imagines that his wife is with him and freezing him with a kiss. "*La douceur le tuait.*"

The doctor in *Poussière sur la Ville* returns, against the advice of a friendly priest, to the ghastly little dust-covered mining town in which he has set up his practice but in which he has been humiliated by the unfaithfulness and suicide of his wife, so that he cannot expect, after this, to be anything but badly received. The priest, Père Dupas, in *Le Temps des Hommes* has fled from his clerical duties when he has had to administer the sacrament to a child who is dying of meningitis. He has been tortured, after the death of the child, by a sense of divine injustice confused with a sense of guilt at having committed the sin of pride because he has appealed to God not to let the child die and so dared to tell Him what to do. When he has buried himself in the woods and associated only with "a brutish humanity," he has come to doubt the sharp distinction, so important for the French

170

Canadian Church, between the soul and the body. Still, hoping to be of some service to a doomed and cowardly murderer, he sticks by him in his flight through the winter woods till the man goes out of his head and makes an attempt to kill him, with the result that, in a tussle for the gun, the priest shoots the man he has been trying to help. He is left at the end with a frozen foot, which may be gangrenous and have to be amputated. This Père Dupas, an Existentialist persister, combines also the recurrent Canadian figure of the fugitive into the wilds with the priest who has a hard row to hoe. But this priest points a moral, not localized, in relation to the Christian religion. The book has something in common with both Graham Greene's *The Power and the Glory* and Edwin O'Connor's *The Edge of Sadness*. Langevin has, however, put Père Dupas in a situation even more baffling than those of the priests in these other books. Greene's priest is a parishless alcoholic wandering in communist Mexico at a time when the priesthood were persecuted; O'Connor's has pitted himself against a sordid and alien parish where he has for his only companion a simple-minded Polish curate. Père Dupas, who has always been handicapped by an incapacity for human relations, is condemned to a wretched lumber camp in the worst possible season of the year, with a crew of unattractive woodsmen, of whom only two will come back alive. And you have, also, here that other French Canadian specialty, the frustrated love affair, for Dupas is loved by a woman who does not know that he is a priest and that he cannot return her devotion.

171

There is, however, a very strong sex interest in these novels of Langevin, which gives them a kind of vitality that is lacking in so many of the others. He has also published a play, *L'Œil du Peuple* (1957), which deals with the triumph of "sexuality," as it is now so often called. Though it was produced in Montreal and won a prize, this play seems to me unsuccessful, and is in any case of purely local interest—a satire on French Canadian prudery. A Parti d'Épuration is about to win an election and impose its puritanical restrictions, but, because of flagrant scandals on the part of the staff and the megalomania of the leader, the organization goes to pieces, and the only way to save it from bankruptcy is to allow its headquarters to be turned into a brothel by a Consortium des Plaisirs.

Today, French Canadian literature, in spite of its almost unillumined gloominess, is undoubtedly more alive and interesting than it has ever been before. (In a chronology compiled by Mlle Lapointe of the important events in this literature, most of them are seen to date from the middle thirties of this century.) What, one wonders, is to be its future? It has considerable obstacles to surmount. It is cut off from the mother culture. The French Canadians, for the reasons mentioned, have something of a grudge against France; and, on their side, the French are imperturbably snobbish in matters of language and speech. Even the scripts of Canadian documentary films have sometimes to be put into Parisian French before they can be shown in France, and a young Canadian told me that on one occasion—though he was working on the Encyclopédie Larousse—a Frenchman he had met in Paris suggested that they might better speak English, since the Parisian would no doubt not be able to understand the Canadian's French. At the same time, the French Canadians have not yet been able to impose on a wider audience—as the Americans have to some extent done —a literary language of their own. When they make use of their own vocabulary, they are likely to give rise to misunderstandings. For example, in my copy of *Bonheur d'Occasion*, printed by Flammarion in Paris, I find the following detail in a description: "*la tranquillité du majestueux original qui vient le soir s'abreuver entre les roseaux.*" The explanation of this strange statement is, I suppose, that whereas a moose in France is called "*un élan canadien*," in Canada it is "*un orignal*," a word unfamiliar to the French, which the Paris printer and proofreader could not be expected to recognize. A famous example of comic misunderstanding occurs in an English translation of the same novel. As the story is sometimes told—as it is by Harry Lorin Binsse in an article in the Montreal *Star*—an account of a Quebec blizzard begins with the following sentence: "*Vers huit heures du soir, la poudrerie éclata.*" I find that in my Paris edition the sentence reads "*se déchaînait,*" not "*éclata,*" and I wonder whether Mme Roy may not, for this edition, have changed the verb in order not to mislead foreign readers. In any case, the English translator, not knowing that in French Canada "*une poudrerie*" is "a blizzard," made it "Toward eight o'clock in the evening the powerworks exploded." No powderworks

173

has yet been mentioned, but the explosion is given for the moment a certain plausibility by the description that follows of cracking trees, rattling shutters and tearing roofs. The powderworks disaster, however, is never mentioned again. I find also in the speeches of Réal Caouette, the French Canadian prophet of Social Credit, the following local words, unintelligible outside French Canada: "*enfarger*," which means to take a pratfall, and "*suiveux*," which means a yes-man, an obsequious follower.

In Canada, I was made aware as I never had been before of the importance of nationalism as a stimulating force to literature. It was true of most of our own best writers till after the Civil War that they were occupied in one way or another with the attempt to give America an identity—by inventing a legendary past, by idealizing an imperfect present or by prophesying a transcendent future. All these writers had a national mission. But in English-speaking Canada no such mission was felt, because no such independence and no such unity had been achieved. The English writing of Canada is scattered all across the continent; it has no center, no organic development. In French Canada, on the other hand, the literature has kept pace with the nationalist cause, and it is evidently taken more seriously than its English-speaking neighbors take theirs. The tone of an English Canadian writing on English Canadian literature is likely to be "Well, perhaps we ought to take stock and find out what we've really got"; the tone of a French Canadian writing on his is one of almost anguished solicitude. One thinks of small nationalities, like Ireland and Hungary, in which the literature has been largely inspired by a movement for national independence and, in turn, has provided an active ferment in the political life of the people. French Canadian literature, besides, is concentrated in a much smaller area than is the writing of the English Canadians. In spite of the curious disassociation of the writers from one another that one observes, though to a lesser extent, in French as well as in English Canada, one finds oneself here in a world which, though much more inbred and limited, is subjected to a higher emotional pressure—a society in which the writers have the stimulus of a common discontent, a common interest in preserving their language, and the excitement of a common animosity.

3

THE NATIONALISTS. It is enough to have read the novels and the other works described above to recognize that the life of French Canada is constricted and full of frustrations. One outlet for the younger generation has been the anticlerical movement—the rebellion against the tyranny of the Church, partly encouraged by Pope John's reforms. Another has been a vigorous reaction against pressures imposed by the English.

The antagonism toward the English does not date in its more virulent form from the "Conquest" of 1760. The French Canadians did not at first much feel themselves crowded by their conquerors. They were actually in a majority in the part of Canada where they lived, and the English let them alone. Wolfe's soldiers became thoroughly Gallicized, and some families with Scottish names are at the present time unable to speak English. But the Protestants soon moved into eastern Canada, and they made themselves the masters of its commerce. The French were ill-equipped to deal with them. They found themselves at a disadvantage in not possessing a bourgeoisie. After the victory of the British and the conceding of French Canada to the English by Louis XV at the Peace of Paris, the French administrators and *commerçants*, who could no longer look forward to careers in French Canada, for the most part packed up and went home. They left a few seignorial estates, a small professional class, an unambitious and illiterate peasantry and a priesthood that came to be the mainstays of the otherwise unenlightened parishes. It was inevitable that—with little other guidance—this priesthood should dominate French Canada, while a hard-headed business world was growing up both around and within it. The first serious rebellion of the French was that led by Louis-Joseph Papineau in 1837. Papineau was a spirited and brilliant man who had for years been Speaker of the colonial Assembly. This local governing body had been struggling with the British Crown for the control of Canadian revenue and for an elective Legislative Council modelled on the American Senate. It had already caused the British government to drop a bill for a union of French and English Canada, which would have restricted the freedom of the Catholic Church, made English the official language and imposed so high a property franchise that most of the French inhabitants would not have been able to vote. The new governor of Lower Canada (Quebec) refused the Assembly's demands. Papineau had been working with the leader of the reform party of Upper Canada (Ontario), but three Frenchmen had been killed by English troops in an election riot of 1832, and he became more and more a French patriot. He now advocated escaping from the British by having

180

French Canada annexed to the American Union. He instigated armed resistance to the government, and a battle took place in Montreal. The "Patriots" were defeated and Papineau took refuge in the United States. Lord Durham, who at this moment was appointed Governor General of British North America, had twelve of the rebels executed and the rest deported in order to save them from death. He made a report to the Crown that was to become one of the most famous documents in Canadian history. Durham was a Whig, rather far to the Left, who was sympathetic to the colonists and who carefully studied their problems. He approved of the French priesthood, but he thought the French Canadians very primitive, and decided that the best that could be done for them was to have them become assimilated to the English civilization. He complained that he had not been able to discover that French Canada had produced any culture of its own. (Professor Lower, in commenting on the Durham report—his summary of which I have here been paraphrasing—subjoins, apropos of this complaint: "His search would have been even more barren in English Canada.") One passage in Lord Durham's report has by this time become rather hackneyed, but it is worth noting here as an early recognition of the split in Canadian society: "I expected to find a contest between a government and a people: I found two nations warring in the bosom of a single state. I found a struggle not of principles but of races."

Growing fear of the expansion of the United States, after the victory over the South in the Civil War, impelled the Canadian provinces to unite under a kind of constitution—the British North America Act—in the Confederation of 1867; but a recrudescent nationalist feeling on the part of the French Canadians was aroused by the execution of Louis Riel in 1885, and it has been kept alive ever since. Riel, a French half-breed with Irish blood, had been the leader, in 1870, of a rebellion of the colony of Roman Catholic half-breeds at Fort Garry, now Winnipeg, against the inroads of surveyors from the East. The territorial rights in this region of the Hudson's Bay Company had just been transferred to the Dominion of Canada, and the population of the colony was afraid of being dispossessed. Riel had already succeeded in keeping out a newly appointed governor, and he had set up a provisional government of his own. This government court-martialled and shot a young Orangeman who refused to accept its authority, and a military force was sent out that unseated it and drove Riel, like Papineau, to take refuge in the United States. But he very soon returned, and, in the seventies, was twice elected to Parliament and twice expelled. He went to live in Montana, and then was recalled to Canada, in 1885, to head another rebellion, this time in the Saskatchewan Valley, by another half-breed colony which was afraid that English settlers would take their lands. This insurrection, too, was put down, and Riel was tried for treason. The jury, which found him guilty, recommended mercy, but the revengeful anti-Papist Orangemen, remembering the death of their co-religionist, demanded that Riel be hanged. The execution was twice postponed, but the Ulstermen at last prevailed. A great meeting of French Canadians was thereupon assembled in Montreal, at which a French politician named Honoré Mercier called for a national party. Riel became a symbol of French revolt. Mercier was made Premier of Quebec in 1887 and lasted till 1891. He called his ministry a "national government," and attempted to put through a bill—furiously opposed by the Orangemen—to compensate the Jesuit Order for the estates that had been taken from them by the English. The situation was further exacerbated, in 1894-96, by the problem of the Manitoba schools. The French in Manitoba had by this time been reduced to a minority by the newly arrived English and these latter set up their own school system, subsidized by the state, and refused to grant state support for French-speaking Catholic schools. The crisis was met by Sir Wilfrid Laurier, the French Canadian federal Prime Minister, through a compromise that gave the Catholics not separate schools but some control over their children's education. The Quebec Roman Catholic Church did not want to accept this and, says Lower, treated Laurier, a Catholic, as if he were the Antichrist. In this quandary, he appealed to Rome. The Orangemen loudly cried out against "papal domination" in Canada, and the Pope, in an encyclical "in carefully guarded language . . . enjoined his bishops to quiet down." "The incident," says Professor Lower, "must have impressed on the Prime Minister what he already no doubt knew, that it is not easy to govern a country, part of whose people are more British than the King and part more Catholic than the Pope."

So much will be enough to show the kind of wrestling between the two peoples which has been going on in Canada for decades. At the time of the Boer War, when the imperialism of Britain was booming, its spirit was communicated to English Canada, which enthusiastically sent troops to South Africa; but the French, who regarded themselves as victims of British imperialism, resisted and followed the course that had been indicated by Mercier in organizing a nationalist movement which opposed the involvement of French Canadians in what they regarded as England's predatory wars. In the first war against Germany, the French at first seemed to be supporting it as strongly as the English did, but the belligerent pressure of the Protestant clergy, the tactlessness of the English Canadians (who kept calling the French slackers), the fact that the language of command was English and an unfortunately timed decision on the part of the Ottawa government to make English the primary language of education, finally, in 1917, the passage of a conscription act—all this had the cumulative effect of violently antagonizing the French Canadians, who, not having been rescued by the French of France at the time they had been fighting the English invaders, were not necessarily eager to risk their lives in order to rescue the French from the Germans. The French Canadians were also opposed—though not to the same degree—to taking part in the Second World War, and the Liberal Prime Minister, Mackenzie King, used furtive and rather disingenuous methods to get by with a commitment to conscription. The French nationalists were still resisting it in the provincial elections of 1944, but by 1945 it was evident that the war would very soon be over, and the issue was left unsettled.

The nationalist movement in Canada has recently entered on a new phase, which has involved in some quarters the proposal that Quebec Province and possibly New Brunswick should split off from the Confederation and set up as a separate country called Laurentie, and which has even, on the part of extremists, given rise to a campaign of violence. This revolt was an immediate consequence of the death of Maurice Duplessis, who had succeeded for more than eighteen years, 1936-39 and 1944-59, in exercising almost dictatorial powers as Premier of the Province of Quebec, and in order to understand what has been happening there it is necessary to study the career of this ruthless, almost feudally reactionary, and provincially exceptional man. This has been made conveniently easy by the recent publication of two books on Duplessis: *The Chief*, by Leslie Roberts, and *Le Vrai Visage de Duplessis*, by Pierre Laporte. The first of these is a political biography by a veteran liberal journalist, who writes without partisanship, and the second a collection of anecdotes and first-hand impressions by a reporter for the Montreal newspaper *Le Devoir*, which one imagines M. Laporte had been filing away through the years.

Maurice LeNoblet Duplessis, born in 1890, was the

son of a lawyer-politician, who eventually went to the bench of the Superior Court of Quebec, and the scion of a *maison seigneuriale*, with all the assumptions of superiority which this social position implied. He stood high in his Catholic college and won a prize for a thesis on "The Theology of St. Thomas," but he is believed, after leaving this school, never to have read a book, and—he never cared to visit France—was content to write and speak bad French. He had the utmost contempt for literature, and could always bring a laugh from his audience by saying of someone, "*Ça, c'est un poète!*" It was he who banished Jean-Charles Harvey from Quebec, even after the author of *Les Demi-Civilisés* had already been dismissed from his paper and buried in a government office. He was equally contemptuous of science, to the degree that he refused to listen to the opinions of engineers on mineralogical problems. He had no interest other than politics and, while still at the seminary, is said to have announced, "I shall be the Premier of Quebec," and, at law school, "Some day *I'll* run this province and make Ottawa listen!" He concentrated so single-mindedly on his chosen field that he became, at thirty-seven, Conservative deputy to the Provincial Parliament from his birthplace, Trois-Rivières, and, nine years later, Premier of Quebec.

Duplessis's declared objective through the whole of his political career was the triumph of French Canadian nationalism. He ostentatiously defended the "autonomy" of the Province of Quebec from the "centralization" of Ottawa, and even when he was leasing out Quebec to American and British Canadian interests, these professions were believed by the rustics upon whom he depended for his strength. From the moment of his entry into public life, Duplessis was arrogantly unscrupulous. He got himself elected to Parliament by allying himself with a group of young Liberals who were working against the antiquated machine of the Liberal Premier Taschereau. Taschereau had succeeded, over a period of fifteen years, in consolidating a government hierarchy based on favoritism and seniority in office; there were forty-five of his relatives on the payroll. Duplessis, though a member of the Conservative Party, combined with these Liberal reformers in a Union Nationale. He went after Taschereau tooth and nail, and uncovered scandalous irregularities in the proceedings of the Committee of Public Accounts. When he revealed that Taschereau's brother had deposited to his private bank account the interest from public funds, the Premier was forced to resign, and the Union Nationale was able to swing the election that followed and to instal Duplessis as Premier. He immediately proceeded to disassociate himself from his young Liberal friends by deliberately alienating them or assigning them to minor positions. It had been one of his campaign promises that the Union Nationale would break the power of the public-utilities trust; but when the young Liberal leaders complained that he was not doing anything about this, he would sneer at those "imbeciles" who thought that "politics consists of keeping promises." He did relieve the destitution of the farmers—on whom he mainly

187

depended for support—by providing them with low-interest loans. His method with these peasants was simple. He would go into the country among them and put on an excellent show, with brass bands and free liquor and a rally in the public square, at which he would assure them that he had pledged himself to defend Quebec Province against Communism, against the "foreigner" and the urban exploiter. If they wanted a highway paved or a bridge to replace a ferry, they had only to come to *him*—that is, to signify their wishes by voting for the Union Nationale. If they did not so vote, they would find that they did not get any improvements. The public roads that were otherwise well maintained would be left with unimproved stretches where they ran through constituencies that had voted Liberal, and Highway 9, between Quebec and Montreal, of which only one lane had been completed by the Liberals and which led through St. Hyacinthe, the home of one of Duplessis's opponents, was allowed to have a dangerous six-inch drop at the side of the completed surface.

In the elections of November, 1939, Duplessis and his group were defeated. It was the critical moment of the Second World War, and the issue was Canadian conscription. Duplessis, in the *fougue* of one of his speeches, had made a very serious *faux pas*. "Quebec," the Premier had declaimed, "will never be the creature of Ottawa. . . . A vote for Maurice Duplessis and his candidates will be a vote for our autonomy and against conscription. A vote against Maurice Duplessis or any of his candidates will be a vote for participation, assimilation and centralization." "Participation" was the word that ruined him. The conclusion was drawn that his stand was not merely against conscription but against taking part in the war, and to some kind of participation the Mackenzie King government was already committed. Duplessis, as a result of this, was obliged to go into a retirement that lasted for four years. But he also went into training for his eventual return to power. He seems to have had a kind of collapse, and though he is said, in his earlier period, to have indulged in a somewhat reckless conviviality, he now adopted a more wholesome regime, which was strictly non-alcoholic—he drank nothing but orange juice—and which he adhered to all the rest of his life. His habits became almost ascetic. In 1944, he got himself reëlected, on the strength of an attack on the labor unions and "Socialism in all its forms," which won for him the approval of English business, and he also improved his standing by resorting to a more moderate position than the intransigent Bloc Populaire, then led by André Laurendeau, which was still opposing conscription. He now devoted all his energies to maintaining himself in power with a merciless elimination of anyone who tried to check him that recalls the overweening ambition—if not quite the self-mortifications—of the seventeenth-century Bishop Laval. Maurice Duplessis never married. He took a suite in the Château Frontenac and he remained in it all the rest of his life. He would emerge and walk to the Parliament Buildings at half past eight every morning and return at the end of the day—as a rule, to spend his evenings alone. He insatiably read the papers and then threw them down beside his chair, where no one was allowed to touch them till his secretary picked them up. His only pastime was playing the phonograph—as M. Laporte says, "*à tue-tête*." He had few friends and almost never saw anyone except to talk politics. He would occasionally entertain distinguished visitors, but a certain lack of cordiality is indicated by his reception of Pierre Mendès-France, then Prime Minister of the Fourth Republic. "How long have you been in my office, *Monsieur le Premier Ministre?*" Mendès-France consulted his watch: "I'm not sure. I think about twenty minutes." "Are you sure that the government hasn't changed in your country?" Duplessis gave a great shout of laughter, which the company did not echo. No fear of *his* government's changing! He had created for himself a role as the master of a docile machine that, even with such examples as Tammany before us, seems rather astonishing in North America. Duplessis rarely took a vacation, and when he did he always kept in close touch with Quebec. He never delegated any authority, and was said to have "a portable government." He was never to travel in Canada any further west than Toronto.

Duplessis had piercing and expressive eyes, which made people lose countenance when they came into his presence, and a long and crooked nose, which was much caricatured in the press, and about which he seems to have become almost as self-conscious as Jimmy Durante has been of his. When he had sent for a former opponent, who did not appear in his office

190

until after he had been summoned several times, the Chief greeted him with *"Pourquoi ne venais-tu pas? Avais-tu peur de mon nez?"* Even people who disapproved of him were aware of his personal magnetism. His vitality was immense. He easily recuperated from fatigue, and when asked how he was would answer, *"Je suis dangereusement bien."* He was surrounded entirely by yes-men, and if anyone disagreed with him, that official was discarded and his future was closed. On one occasion, at a meeting of the Cabinet, he snapped at a colleague who had queried some decision, "I took you out of the gutter. Keep your mouth shut or I'll put you back where I found you!" In his second administration, he made hash of parliamentary and departmental procedure. In the Legislature, he would audibly coach the speakers or speak for them or interrupt them and make them sit down. The Speaker of the House did not dare to give any delegate the floor without a signal from Duplessis. He enjoyed humiliating his colleagues, all of whom he seems always to have *tutoyéd*—one supposes they had to call him *vous*—and of whom he was frankly contemptuous, saying, *"Sans moi ils ne valent pas cher!"* He was much addicted to crude puns. To an undersecretary described by Laporte as "both cultivated and distinguished"—afterwards ambassador to Spain—who had to deliver to Duplessis at some ceremony the Great Seal of the Province of Quebec, he announced in a voice loud enough to be heard through the whole hall, *"Le petit sot portant le Grand Sceau."* Later on, on some other occasion, this official remarked to Duplessis, *"Saviez-vous, Monsieur le Premier Ministre, qu'autrefois en Angleterre le gardien du Grand Sceau devait coucher avec le Grand Sceau?" "Je ne sais pas. Je sais toutefois qu'il y a longtemps déjà que Madame Bruchési couche avec le grand . . . sot de la province!"* He went over the heads of departments and sometimes did not even consult them in making decisions about matters for which they were supposed to be responsible. He somewhat offset his bullying highhandedness by a paternalistic concern for the home life of those who were resigned to accepting it, sending flowers to their wives in the hospital, making inquiries about the progress of their children, and occasionally replastering a house that seemed on the point of crumbling, but he also took the precaution of keeping dossiers on their misdeeds and scandals. Duplessis was hardly second to Stalin in his demand for constant adulation. Pretending to discourage praise, he always insisted on homage to the beneficent omnipotence of his government. "Does the deputy forget to thank the government?" he would remind at the end of a speech, or "Has the deputy something to say?" "Get up," he would sharply prompt him.

The policies of Duplessis in office displayed the same outrageous insolence. (In describing them, I shall run together the events of his two administrations.) He did not hesitate to take measures or to put through laws which he must have known to be unconstitutional but of which he could be sure that it would take a long time to have their unconstitutionality declared. (It is a to us strange feature of Canadian government, both federal and provincial, that a Prime Minister may allot to himself a post in his own Cabinet, and Duplessis had made himself Attorney General.) The most notorious of these extra-constitutional exploits was the Padlock Law of 1937, "An Act Respecting Communistic Propaganda," which, without defining what this was, made it illegal to publish anything "propagating or tending to propagate Communism or Bolshevism," and gave authority to close any building in which anything of the kind was supposed to take place. This remained on the books twenty years and was used for all sorts of suppressions—police raids that confiscated newspapers and lockings of people out of their lodgings. The boast that he had purged Quebec of Communism became one of Duplessis's great appeals to both the Church, which was afraid of its atheism, and the industrials, who were afraid of its agitators. His "war without mercy" on Jehovah's Witnesses also strengthened his position with the Church. He prosecuted over sixteen hundred members of this fanatical sect, which at most was only a minor nuisance, on charges that ranged from disturbing the peace to engaging in seditious activities. An Italian restaurant keeper, Frank Roncarelli, who had been supplying bail for the Witnesses had his liquor license revoked and his entire stock of liquor confiscated. This gave rise to a vigorous protest on the part of English-speaking Montrealers, but it was not until five years later that Roncarelli was able to get any satisfaction in having this injustice righted. He had brought suit against Duplessis, and eventually a judge with a Scottish name censured the

Quebec Premier for giving orders to the Liquor Commission and for failing to disqualify himself in his role of Attorney General in a case in which he figured as a private citizen. MacKinnon awarded Roncarelli $8,123 in damages. Since Duplessis appealed against this and Roncarelli, too, appealed for more damages, the case went on for eight years more, at the end of which time the Supreme Court of Canada decided against Duplessis and awarded to Roncarelli $33,123, plus interest and costs. The same court, two years before, had declared the Padlock Law unconstitutional, in connection with the case of a man—ironically enough, a Communist—whom the police had locked out of his apartment. Both these cases were argued by Mr. Frank R. Scott, Professor of Law at McGill University, the relative mildness of whose satirical verse I have mentioned in discussing Canadian poetry but whose effectiveness as a fighter for civil rights is by no means open to such criticism.

In the field of education, Duplessis was, in his way, constructive and generous, insofar as he built new schools and increased the grants for schooling, but his way of doing this was still feudal and hence autocratic. He invariably withheld these facilities if any member of a school board voted Liberal, and if the school badly needed anything, the Liberal had to go. I have spoken of his efforts to eliminate from the Laval School of Social Sciences the Dominican Père Lévesque, who has played such an important role in the cultural life of French Canada. Duplessis, as the defender of provincial rights against federal intervention, usually

194

made a point of rejecting federal aid to education, and he refused to receive delegations of students from French Catholic universities who wanted to take advantage of university grants then being offered by Ottawa. On the same grounds, he fought a bill for a national system of employment insurance. In the labor field, while constantly posing as the champion of his own people against alien exploitation, he did everything possible to bring to Quebec English Canadian and American capital by the lure of the local low wages. He declared war on organized labor—jailed labor leaders, incited riots and suppressed many strikes as illegal. Always relying on his popularity with the primitive rural population, Duplessis was so little in touch with the forces of modern industrial society that he could not foresee that this policy was bound to make him unpoular in the cities.

In the case of the great asbestos strike of 1949, this policy cost Duplessis a defeat. The asbestos industry of Quebec at that time produced eighty-five per cent of the world supply of this commodity. At the Johns-Manville Company plant in the town of Asbestos, five thousand workers had walked out, demanding a fifteen-per-cent raise, which would mean a basic raise of a dollar a day—well below, Mr. Roberts tells us, the average wage for Canadian mineworkers—and protection against silicosis, the suffocating lung disease contracted through inhaling the dust from the mills. (One remembers the pernicious atmosphere of the little asbestos mill town in Langevin's *Poussière sur la Ville*.) The employers refused to negotiate, and the strike lasted a hundred and forty-one days. Duplessis first sent in the provincial police, with the intention, apparently, of provoking hostilities, and then, in his capacity as Attorney General, condemned the strike as illegal. The strikers, who had in some way been led to believe that they were threatened with an invasion of strikebreakers protected by armed police, put the town into a state of siege, with the approaches defended by road blocks, and riots broke out against the local police and unknown persons who were thought to be strikebreakers. Seventy-five carloads of provincial police were sent in from the outside. But *Le Devoir* came out on the strikers' side and revealed that the asbestos company was paying each of these policemen fifty dollars a week and that a student demonstration at Laval in sympathy with the strikers had at the last minute been called off by the Rector, under pressure from Duplessis, who had threatened to withhold a grant. The Church, too, now backed the strikers, who belonged to a Catholic union and were led by a devout Catholic. Archbishop Charbonneau of Montreal instructed the parish priests to take up collections for the relief of the strikers, who had by now been almost reduced to starvation. From these and from labor organizations, something between two and three hundred thousand dollars was raised. Even the Montreal city police contributed two hundred dollars. The company settled for a ten-per-cent raise instead of the demanded fifteen, as well as holidays with pay, elimination of asbestos dust and reëmployment—which up to then had been refused by the company—of all workers involved in the strike.

But Archbishop Charbonneau, for his support of the asbestos strikers, was made to pay a terrible price. He had already been out of favor with Duplessis, whom he was said on one occasion to have thrown out of the archiepiscopal palace. For Charbonneau, like Père Lévesque of Laval, had studied sociology, and Duplessis hated sociologists, with their solicitude for the industrial working class. The Archbishop seems the perfect opponent, the spokesman for Christian idealism, which the challenge of Duplessis required, and their conflict became so dramatic that it should surely, at some later period, provide an historical play—of the type of Hochhuth's *The Deputy* or Werfel's *Juarez and Maximilian*—for the French Canadian theater. Certain steps in this tragic drama had till recently remained mysterious; but as a result of persistent inquiry a certain amount of light has been thrown on them by the researches of Mlle Renaude Lapointe, a reporter for the Montreal *Nouveau Journal*, whose articles for this paper have been published in a book, *L'Histoire Bouleversante de Mgr Charbonneau*.

Joseph Charbonneau was the son of an apparently rather well-to-do Ontario farmer who lived on the Ottawa River. He studied at the Catholic University in Washington, D.C., and at the Collège Canadien in Rome. He taught philosophy in Paris at St.-Sulpice and was given an honorary degree in philosophy by Ottawa University. He was made bishop when he was forty-seven, in 1939, and archbishop the following year. He was the first Archbishop of Montreal who had ever come out of Ontario, and this and his early experience of Europe and the United States—his knowledge of the non-Catholic as well as of the non-French Canadian world—had saved him from the provinciality so often characteristic of the Québecois clergy. Charbonneau stands out as a figure with a clear individual outline that differentiates him from the body to which he belonged and to which he must have been something of an alien. He was glad to accept invitations to the festivities of the Irish Catholics—to whom the French were not always friendly—and he even expressed an entirely unorthodox ambition "to be archbishop not only of the Catholics but of all the Montrealers." To the horror of conventional churchmen, he approved the admission of non-Catholics to the trade unions and the workers' coöperatives. He was able, energetic, intelligent, with an authority that derived both from obvious good will and from physical strength and imposing stature, and he made himself much respected in Montreal during the decade of his active ministry.

Charbonneau had been occupied with the problems of the young people who had recently been swarming from the countryside into the cities and finding themselves unemployed or at the mercy of the factory owners. At the time of the asbestos strike, he made the following public statement: "We desire social peace, but we do not want the working class crushed. We are more attached to men than to capital. It is on this

198

Archbishop Charbonneau with Premier Duplessis. From left to right: Antonio Talbot, Duplessis' Minister of Roads, and Romeo Lorrain, his Minister of Public Works. Duplessis is holding a pair of shears to cut the ribbon at the opening of a road or bridge. Note the patch under the arm of Charbonneau's cassock. *Courtesy of the Toronto* Gazette account that the clergy have decided to intervene. We wish to inspire respect for charity and for justice, and we desire to see less respect paid to the interests of money than to the human element." Charbonneau, who had had experience as superior of the Ottawa Grand Séminaire and as principal of the Normal School at Hull, as Archbishop became ex officio Chancellor of Montreal University, in which capacity he raised eleven million dollars, and set out to modernize its curriculum and bring it up to the standards of McGill. He drew up a new charter—unacceptable to Duplessis—which gave the lay members of the faculty more importance in the administration. He obtained the reorganization of several of the departments and approved the introduction of a department of psychology, which included psychoanalysis. Charbonneau did his best to diminish the gap between the educational advantages of English Canada and the relatively scant opportunities afforded by Catholic Quebec. He tried to have two more years added to the courses of the Jesuit college, Loyola, in order that its graduates might not be obliged to go on at such an early age to McGill, and he worked to procure through taxation enough funds to emulate Ontario, where the state provided twelve years of schooling. "Why," he asked, "should our education here not be brought, on an equal basis, within reach of the whole population?" He backed a law making school attendance compulsory, which was put through in the teeth of Duplessis but disregarded when he was reëlected. In a school strike of 1949—which was of course denounced by the Premier—Charbonneau took the side of the teachers. This was the year when he had already supported the strike of the asbestos workers.

He was to last only one year longer as Archbishop of Montreal, after a pastorate of only ten years. Not merely the Premier of Quebec but also the reactionary Archbishop of Rimouski, Mgr Georges Courchesne, had become his implacable enemy. Archbishop Courchesne drew up and himself presented in Rome a list of charges against Charbonneau. The Archbishop of Montreal, according to this memorandum, was "no longer in communion with the hierarchy"; he was "preaching an advanced social Catholicism"; he had "put the Episcopacy in an embarrassing position at the time of the asbestos strike, in view of the fact that the unions had defied the law of the province"; he had "placed the whole clergy in a difficult position as a result of his hostility to the legitimate government of M. Duplessis"; he "had occupied himself with social theses at the expense of his administration and had made too many concessions to the Communists"—i.e., the international unions. Archbishop Charbonneau had also come to be at serious odds with the papal delegate to Ottawa, Mgr Ildebrando Antoniutti, a smooth and noncommittal Italian, to whom the Archbishop's forthrightness was apparently uncongenial. It is claimed by Charbonneau's friends that Duplessis—who had boasted in the provincial Parliament that he "had the clergy eating out of his hand"—brought pressure to bear on Antoniutti, threatening to cut off funds in the Montreal diocese unless Charbonneau were removed.

At any rate, two of Duplessis's ministers were dispatched to Rome for the Holy Year with a mission which one of them told friends was very delicate and which he did not like, and at the beginning of 1950 the Archbishop was notified by the Vatican Secretariat of State, over which the Pope presided, that he was ordered to resign before the end of the month or "accept an apostolic administration," in which last event he would be allowed to stay on, as Charbonneau said, "as a decorative object." He called on Antoniutti, who confirmed the decree of the Vatican. The interview is reported to have been disagreeable. Mlle Lapointe, Charbonneau's biographer, in her effort to get to the bottom of the intrigue which had effected Charbonneau's dismissal, paid a visit to Mgr Antoniutti, then enjoying one of the plums of the Vatican's diplomatic service as the nuncio at Madrid. She found him surrounded, she says, with "masterpieces of Spanish painting, immense Gobelin tapestries, graceful sculptures, a reredos of the old Castilian school," and other objects of luxury. He explained that a papal representative, from the moment he left his post, was unable "to supply information as to events which had occurred during his administration." He assured Mlle Lapointe that he regarded Charbonneau as "a great archbishop," and added that he cherished the memory of this great man's zeal and devotion and that he prayed for him.

In the meantime, Charbonneau had resigned. He had appealed to the Secretariat to no avail; he had written a letter to the Pope petitioning that he be allowed to

201

come to Rome and present his defense in person, and had even made a plane reservation, but Pius XII ignored his request. Cardinal Spellman of New York advised Charbonneau to submit; Mgr Cushing of Boston said, "This is the work of wicked men." Charbonneau seems to have been very innocent, for the blow had been quite unexpected. He had visited Rome in February the year before, and had been told by an ecclesiastic friend that he was constantly under attack and that he ought to take measures to protect himself. He had gone straight to the Vatican Consistory and had been told that there was nothing against him. His Roman friend, however, warned him to be on his guard and advised him to stay on awhile, to get to know some of the subordinate officials and induce them to show him his dossier. But the trusting Charbonneau returned to Montreal and told people that he had made inquiries and been assured that his record was clear. Now, suddenly, he found himself dismissed and directed—which he found distasteful—to pretend that he was doing so on account of his health, which at that time was notably robust. He was invested with the bogus and humiliating rank of "Titular Archbishop of Bosphorus"—whereupon he removed his archiepiscopal ring—and was shipped off to the opposite edge of the continent, to Victoria in British Columbia. He was smuggled away at dawn on a plane, with two bags and less than seventy dollars in cash—he had given the rest of his money to his diocese. On account of his great popularity, the authorities did everything possible to prevent his departure from being known and did not announce his resignation till a week after he was gone. A clamor then was raised in the Canadian press, and the Vatican denied that he had been forced to resign on account of "his supposed anti-capitalist attitude." Six weeks later, in consolation, "for services rendered to the Church," he was awarded the titles of Roman Count and of Assistant to the Pontifical Throne. "They cut off both my legs," he said, "and then give me a gold-headed cane to help me walk."

Charbonneau, arrived in Victoria, was received at the airport and given an apartment in the Mount Saint Mary's Home for the Aged. There this naturally active and strong-willed man was condemned to years of near-vegetation. He took long walks, read a great many books and sent off innumerable letters, smoked incessantly and documented himself on the region to which he had been sent and in which it had been made impossible for him to accomplish anything constructive. A great many people came to see him. Since his departure, his fame had grown. Deprived of his see and in exile, he had almost the prestige of a saint. Eventually, when the chaplain of the Home was away, he was asked to visit the sick in his stead. When this chaplain had returned, Charbonneau was offered the chaplaincy of the Sisters of Saint Anne, which was conveniently just across the street. "I'm finishing my ministry," he said, "just as I began it—teaching the catechism." He died in November, 1959, as the result of a car accident, a coronary thrombosis, bladder trouble and diabetes. It was as if his physique had collapsed when it was prevented from carrying out his purpose.

The doctor had made him stop smoking. "*Que je m'ennuie donc!*" he sighed while he was waiting to die in the hospital. The body of Charbonneau was sent home to Montreal, where a hugely attended Mass was said for him in the cathedral. In spite of defeat and death, his moral example was lasting. Joseph Charbonneau was to come to stand as a pioneer and martyr of Church reform. The nonsectarianization of the unions was very soon to be accepted; the laicizing of education was soon to be undertaken on a scale that the Archbishop may never have imagined.

But, even before Charbonneau's fall, Duplessis had found himself in trouble. A serious scandal had broken and had led to the sensational discovery that the Duplessis organization was committed to a system of corruption beside which the peculations of its predecessor, the Taschereau administration, which Duplessis had once exposed, seemed relatively trivial and venial. But had not Duplessis, after all, been following Taschereau's example with more boldness and fewer scruples? It was inevitable, one supposes, in still semi-feudal Canada, that any government, however democratic in theory, should become authoritarian, and authoritarianism had inevitably led to plunder. Two abbés, in 1956, had circulated a daring pamphlet that attacked the electoral practices of l'Union Nationale, and hence, since the Duplessis machine had just been reëlected, the methods of the government itself. It showed that not only the laity but the Church organizations, and in some cases even the clergy, had been taking bribes to vote for the government. And now, in 1958, *Le Devoir* made the accusation that at least six of Duplessis's ministers, and perhaps Duplessis himself, had taken advantage of private knowledge of the sale of government property—the distribution facilities of the Hydro-Quebec Corporation having been sold to a privately owned company, the Quebec Natural Gas Corporation, which was now making excess profits by charging excessive rates. These officials were supposed to have enriched themselves to the extent of twenty million dollars by acquiring shares at low prices before the sale had been announced and then cashing in on their increased value. The Premier sued the paper, but the main accusations were proved. An investigation conducted by a Royal Commission of Inquiry uncovered a huge system of graft. Even the hospitals and sanatoriums had been used by the Department of Health as indirect channels for transmitting large gratuitous sums which did not appear on their books. Two of Duplessis's principal henchmen—his treasurer, whose function it was to assign government contracts and who had been selling them for party contributions, and his Minister of Colonization, who was more realistically known to the press as the "Minister of Constituencies and Elections" —were especially censured by the Commission's report.

Duplessis did not live to see all this. He must have known that his officials were grafting and selling government contracts, but he apparently had not known about the deal with the Natural Gas Corporation. He was furious with the guilty ministers: *"Vous, vous êtes foutus dans le pétrin, laissez-moi tenter de vous en sortir.*" The situation provoked one of his brutal snubs, which has since become a catchphrase in French Canada. On the occasion of some public gathering, when he was detonating against *Le Devoir*, and his loyal Solicitor General made an attempt to reinforce his remarks, the Prime Minister shut him up with "*Toé, tais-toé, Rivard!*" (*Toé* is peasant French for *toi.*) There was no evidence that Duplessis himself had ever made any illicit profit. He was comfortably well-off, had no luxurious tastes and was casual about money. When his will came to be probated, it was found that he had nothing but a few paintings, which had been given him and which he left to the province, and a few thousand dollars, which he left to his relatives. He had cared about nothing but power. He died in September of '59, perhaps shamed and broken like Harding. On a visit to the iron pits on the Labrador-Quebec border which he had sold to a Canadian mining group and which had then been rebought by an American company but of the vigorous development of which Duplessis was extremely proud, he had a series of cerebral hemorrhages. In a few days the Chief was dead. He was then in his seventieth year. When, after the first of these strokes, he was admonished by the doctors to be careful, he had retorted, "*Je ne suis pas une catin, moi!*" His funeral, in the cathedral of Trois-Rivières, was attended by hundreds of weeping women.

———

THE SEPARATISTS. The death of Duplessis and the destruction of the Duplessis machine, which followed the exposure of its practices, had a liberating effect on French Canada and inaugurated a new phase of the nationalist movement. What Duplessis had come to mean for the young, for the elements who were growing impatient with the feudal regime in Quebec, which masked, as they thought, the surrender to English and American interests, is best illustrated by a famous editorial written by André Laurendeau for *Le Devoir* on the occasion of one of its reporters' being ejected from a Duplessis press conference:

Quebec's Anglophones behave like the British in one of their African colonies.

The British are too wise, politically; they rarely destroy the political institutions of a conquered country. They surround the Negro King, but they let him behave as he pleases. Occasionally he will be permitted to cut off heads if it is customary. It would never occur to them to demand of a Negro King that he conform to the high moral and political standards of the British.

The Negro King must collaborate and protect the interests of the British. With this taken care of, the rest counts for little. Does the little king violate the rules of democracy? Well, what could one expect from such a primitive creature?

I do not attribute these attitudes to the English minority of Quebec. But things go on as if some of its leaders believed in the theory and practice of the Negro King. They pardon in M. Duplessis, chief of Quebec's natives, what they would not stand for in one of their own. [Translation, slightly revised, from *The Quebec Revolution*, by Hugh Bingham Myers.]

The comparison of the French Canadians with the natives of African colonies was given a certain appropriateness by the insulting habit of the British Canadians of ordering the French to "talk white" when they failed to express themselves in English. This pretension of the English that the French belong to an inferior race whose language they cannot be expected to bother with has been carried to preposterous lengths. Even among tolerably well-educated people, you rarely hear an English Canadian make any attempt to pronounce a French name correctly. I found in Montreal that when I called up the offices of *Maclean's Magazine* and wanted to speak to the editor of the French edition, I could not ask for Monsieur Lapointe if the English-speaking staff were to know whom I meant but had to call him Mister Lapoint, with the "point" pronounced as in "ball point." Even among literary people, the name of the novelist Gabrielle Roy is likely to be pronounced like Rob Roy. And one even finds Francophile English Canadians who adore the French of France—painting, literature, châteaux, cuisine and all the rest—but are contemptuous of the French of French Canada, a country they seem hardly to have visited.

It became very plain, after Duplessis's death, that French Canada wanted no more *rois nègres*. What it wanted was independence of the British—independence, in a sense, of its own past. In this past, the Catholic Church had always been a conservative force; it had inhibited social change. But Pope John had come to the Vatican the year before Duplessis's extinction, and Cardinal Léger of Quebec was one of the chief agents of Pope John's reforms. Archbishop Charbonneau had been justified. French Canadians now had the

208

feeling that the brakes had been taken off; they were free to possess their own soul. (In an article in the Toronto monthly *Saturday Night*, the novelist Roger Lemelin has announced that the School of Social Sciences at Laval University, which was founded by Père Lévesque and which was so fought by Duplessis and the conservative element in the Church, now exercises "complete intellectual control in Quebec and partial control in Ottawa.") French Canadian nationalism now became revolutionary. Lemelin, in answer to a question as to why "La Famille Plouffe" had been dropped as a television soap opera, replied, "Do you not see that they have been killed by this . . . revolution, which has meant that Quebec will not allow such characters . . . to be presented now to English-speaking Canada because the new French Canadian is ashamed of them?" And the separatist movement was launched.

This movement has, however, taken no clear line. It has involved a great many groups, and the relations between these groups have been complicated. The situation is further confused by the simultaneous crisis of the Church. In Quebec, one can be liberal in regard to the Church but entirely conservative in politics. One can be a nationalist and yet not a separatist. The word "nationalist" may be used to cover anything from Duplessis to the youthful terrorists, of whom few nationalists or even separatists approve. Among the separatists who want French Canada to break off from the Confederation and set up as an independent country, there are serious differences of opinion as to how this independence is to be achieved. Some advocate a separatist party—the moderate Rassemblement pour l'Indépendance Nationale—which will recruit through public meetings and printed publicity, and eventually vote for separation. But how can one reach the people, who only yesterday were voting for Duplessis, how explain to them the wretchedness of their situation? The "colonialists," according to the separatists, are in control of the channels of communication: radio, television, the popular press. They make separatist sentiments dangerous because they dismiss or refuse to employ any person who is known to entertain them. Other separatists object that to resign oneself to constitutional methods is to recognize the Confederation, which is a part of the colonial system that French Canada ought not to accept. Why not, then, appeal to the United Nations, which has a decolonization committee and which includes several new decolonized African states? Or resort to illegal methods—acts of civil disobedience, obstructive demonstrations; if necessary, open violence? If Quebec resorted to force, would the federal government in Ottawa dare to call out the Army against it? The United States has a large stake in "colonialized" French Canada, as it did in pre-Castro Cuba, and it is afraid of the tendency toward nationalization represented by Hydro-Electric and the proposals of some of the separatists, but, having failed to suppress Castro, it is, they think, extremely improbable that we should attempt to invade Canada. In any case, it has been suggested by one of the separatists, André d'Allemagne, that it would only be necessary for French Canada to sink a couple of ships in the St. Lawrence Seaway to bring its neighbors to terms.

It is difficult to disentangle the various strands of the separatist movement or to see what direction it is taking. There does not seem to be any strong leadership. Even M. Marcel Chaput, who has been one of the most active and articulate of the separatists, has said recently that "the movement for independence reminds me of a horse whose rider has lost the reins: it is going along by itself." And—according to statistics compiled by *Maclean's Magazine*—it consists of only thirteen per cent of the population of French Canada. Forty-three per cent, says *Maclean's*, want to preserve the Confederation, twenty-three per cent are undecided, and twenty-one per cent do not know that the movement exists. In Canada as a whole, the ripples from the "Quebec revolution" grow fainter the farther away one gets from Quebec. Already, one finds in Toronto, the crisis seems rather remote. There is a tendency to grumble and brush it off. In Manitoba, St. Boniface is a French-speaking suburb of Winnipeg, the descendants of the colony defended by Riel, and there are eighty thousand French-speaking inhabitants in the province, but the ancestors of fifteen or twenty per cent of these came straight to Manitoba from France and have no real connection with Quebec, and as one goes farther west, the awareness of Quebec becomes dim. A French Canadian journalist, Mme Solange Chaput-Rolland, has written that, on a lecture trip in which she had intended "to talk about the current upheaval in Quebec"—though she is not, she says, a separatist—she found that "beyond Winnipeg . . . the very existence of Quebec becomes a sort of myth, a folklore of trappers and traders. Please don't think I am exaggerating; between one city and the next I was obliged to rewrite my lectures, to change my speeches so as to talk not about a revolution in Quebec but literally about the fact that Quebec is *there*." Though Maillardville, in British Columbia, has a population of six thousand French, it is difficult to make this province on the Pacific Coast understand why it should be compelled, as the nationalists demand, to have its children learn French at school.

The nationalists and the separatists differ widely about their aims as well as about their methods. Nothing enrages a French Canadian possessed by the spirit of the nationalist movement so much as to be asked by an English Canadian, "But what is it exactly you want?" The regulation answer to this is "To be masters in our own house." But what do they mean by that? I shall not try to review all the programs advanced by different groups and different individuals. Some idea of the opposite poles between which the controversy vibrates may be conveyed by summarizing two pamphlets by two very able publicists of strongly contrasting temperaments and antithetical views: *Pourquoi Je Suis Séparatiste*, by Marcel Chaput, published in 1961, and *Pourquoi Je Suis Antiséparatiste*, by Jean-Charles Harvey, written in answer to Chaput and published the following year.

M. Chaput, though he makes an effort to guard him-

Marcel Chaput. *Photograph by Canada Wide Feature Service*

self against excess—rabid hatred of the British, incitement to violence—is not free from the single-track fanaticism that is likely to be generated by nationalist movements. He strikes one as the kind of man who never thinks of anything but his cause and who cannot look at anything else except to see it in relation to that. Marcel Chaput is forty-five years old, a chemist by profession. Till recently, he worked on chemical-warfare research with the Defense Research Board in Ottawa. But he became involved in the separatist movement, to the detriment, according to the Board, of his laboratory activities. When he was refused leave of absence to go to Quebec for a conference that had been organized by the students of Laval to discuss "The Canadian Experiment, Success or Failure?," this did not deter him from attending, and in consequence he was suspended for two weeks. The Board regarded his separatist activities as bordering on the treasonable. Chaput has made an attempt in his pamphlet to reconcile his conflicting loyalties, but this seems not entirely easy. He says that so long as Canada remained a Confederation he was willing, while working for the government, to acknowledge allegiance to the Queen, but that this did not imply that he surrendered the right to question the political institutions of Canada. When he was suspended by the Board, he at once resigned and began working full time for the already existing separatist organization, Le Rassemblement pour l'Indépendance Nationale, of which he became the president. He ran unsuccessfully for Parliament in the election of 1962 on a separatist ticket, then broke with the

R.I.N. to found an organization of his own, Le Parti Républicain du Québec. He has explained to a reporter for *Saturday Night* that the Rassemblement was "too slow. There would be no political party if they had their way. And they are socialist. The word socialist in Quebec . . ." Chaput, the reporter says, shrugged. The aim of the P.R.Q. is to compose a united front of republicans, taking in the Right as well as the Left. In order to appeal to both wings, it combines a guarantee of "free enterprise" with the nationalization of the telephone service and other public utilities. Foreign industries would be seized. In order to raise money for this organization, Chaput has resorted to hunger strikes—living on bread, water and orange juice—during the first of which he stripped away forty of his two hundred and forty-five pounds. By his first strike, which lasted for thirty-three days, he succeeded in getting contributions to the amount of a hundred thousand dollars, but in the second he was less successful. In January, 1964, he resigned, for unknown reasons, from the leadership of his party, and has since then been given little publicity.

French Canada, says M. Chaput, finds itself in an impossible position, politically, socially and commercially. First of all, it is simply nonsense to talk about Canada as a *nation*. What we have is not a *nation* but a *state*. You could have a Canadian nation only by denying the identity of French Canada, which is what the Ottawa government has been doing its best to do and what it will eventually achieve unless immediate steps are taken by French Canadians to defend their identity. The British North America Act was never really accepted by French Canada. It was never put to a vote but imposed by a decree of Westminster. The Confederation is a structure that is purely political and artificial, founded in the first place by force of arms and the helpless submission of the French Canadians. The French Canadians at the present time constitute almost a third of the population of Canada, yet their representation in its economy and government is proportionately infinitesimal: it counts for only ten per cent. When a question is debated in the House of Commons that intimately concerns French Canada, the issue is inevitably decided by the vote of the English majority. When a plebiscite was taken on conscription, the English voted for it while the French voted against, and conscription was of course put over. When a case from the Province of Quebec is brought before the Ottawa Supreme Court, the situation is quite unfair, since it is a question of the problems of a French community being ruled on by English judges. The French Canadians have no adequate means of defending their own interests. The British North America Act has given the federal government the power to reverse the decisions of a province, but the province has no machinery for rejecting a decision of the government.

In the economy of the country as a whole, the same imbalance prevails. Here the proportion of French Canadian participation is closer to five per cent than ten per cent. In the Province of Quebec itself, the French make up eighty-three per cent of the population, yet of its business they hardly control twenty per cent. It is said that only one per cent of the transactions of the Montreal Stock Exchange deals with French Canadian capital. Of the seventeen directors of the Bank of Canada, only one is a French Canadian. There is not one among the seventeen vice-presidents of Canadian National Railways. There is none among the seven top officials of the new Federal Ministry of Forestry, though Quebec includes twenty-five per cent of the exploitable forests of Canada. The province pays to Ottawa in taxes two billion dollars a year and of this gets only five hundred million back.

British Canada is always attempting to disparage the abilities of the French in industry, in technology, in business. M. Chaput, as a chemical engineer, particularly resents this. The French technician or executive, in order to qualify, is almost always at the disadvantage—as the English-speaking one is not—of being obliged to master another language and to make it the vehicle of all his transactions, and if it is a question of being sent out to some non-French region of Canada, he may not want to exile his family to a place where there are no French schools and no churches of his own religion. This problem of language is fundamental. The language of Canadian business is English. But the French Canadian is proud of his language and will not recognize it as a disability. M. Chaput sums up in an eloquent peroration the grievances of the French Canadian: "He is under the impression that he is speaking an international language, and he has 'Speak white' spat in his face. He enters the French university, and he studies American textbooks. . . . He keeps hearing it declared that Canada is an independent country, and he sees the queen of another country on the coinage and on the stamps. . . . He is exhorted to get rid of his inferiority complex, and they tell him he is not mature enough to conduct his own affairs."

Now, M. Chaput declares, the only way to deal with all this is to establish complete independence. The printing of bilingual bank checks (a practice now officially adopted), which figured so long as an issue, is the type of trivial concession that is belatedly being made by the federal authorities in order to keep French Canada quiet: bilingual signs in Ottawa, translation in the House of Commons and in the military services, the appointment of a few French Canadian officials, some extension of fiscal rights. It would not even mean anything vital if the British exploiters of Quebec should go so far—it had been one of the French demands—as to rename the enormous new Queen Elizabeth Hotel the Château Maisonneuve. It would mean nothing if Ottawa agreed—and some steps have been taken in this direction—to reform the Confederation itself. The separatists do not want a reformed Confederation. They want no Confederation at all. So long as French Canadians are stuck halfway between assimilation to the English and the full realization of their own nationality, they can never be anything but mediocre. No: they want independence as a nation—a nation of one tongue, with its own government, its own armed services, its own representation abroad. Why shouldn't they be a nation? Look at Israel's success in a country that for centuries the Jews had not even inhabited.

Since the end of the last war, more than thirty colonies have established themselves as nations with national sovereignties. Half the countries of the United Nations have a smaller population than French Canada. Would this isolate Quebec? No. There would be as much reciprocity in relations with other countries as in the case of any other nation. Would they be letting down the other French Canadians by leaving them in subjection to an alien government? (There are in all, outside Quebec, a million and a half French Canadians in Canada. Besides the groups mentioned above, there are two hundred and thirty thousand Acadians in New Brunswick alone, whom some of the separatists have advocated including in the new Laurentie.) This could to some extent perhaps not be avoided. But a good many of these non-Québecois French have, "tragically," become anglicized. One could always undertake a campaign to bring these exiles back to Quebec—as well as the more than a million who have gone to the United States—and one could supply them with libraries and colleges to reawaken their interest in the mother culture.

As to the political structure of the new Quebec, this is not the time to decide. (We know, however, from a published interview that Chaput is in favor of a "democratic republic," with a president at its head.) The province must first win its independence. Chaput attempts to formulate a program called "Toward Economic Independence," but his proposals are rather vague: "Nationalize the key industries; encourage the industry of transformation; promote the use of French

218

savings banks; obtain investments of capital from various countries rather than from only one . . . elaborate an overall plan . . . profit from the example of other people . . . destroy the pernicious myth that French Canadians have no business sense." But now we come to what even Chaput must recognize as the fundamental problem. "The independence of Quebec is to be desired," yet the problem is "psychological." "In Quebec, it is not force of arms that keeps the people quiet, it is not the barbed wire of the concentration camp that confines it in its present prison; it is something far more serious. It is the will that has been paralyzed. The people could be free but they refuse to believe it. They could be their real self, but they look for excuses to run away." To exhort one's people to re-vindicate their identity, to make themselves French again, is only to treat the symptoms. "Give back to the people their liberty, and half the symptoms will disappear." Yet how is one to give the people back their liberty when they do not even know that they want it? He ends with a burst of oratory: "Peoples hardly emerged from the Stone Age have obtained the independence they desired. And we, French Canadians, a people issued from the great French civilization, children of the colonists and the pioneers who built this country, is it possible that we should not have the courage to will that which we believe desirable, under the fallacious pretext that our independence would not please this or that other country? If that is the attitude of the people from whom I come, I repudiate my origins and hasten to swell the ranks of those who have been assimilated. For it is only that people that wishes to live who merits the privilege of survival." Let us pass to M. Harvey.

Jean-Charles Harvey, who has already been introduced as the author of *Les Demi-Civilisés* and a rebel at forty against constituted authority, is seventy-four today, which may account for his relative conservatism as his partly Scottish blood may account for his relatively favorable view of the British. In his anti-separatist pamphlet, however, he begins by deploring the unwillingness of most of the "Anglophones," after two centuries of living with French neighbors, to attain any mastery of French beyond *"bonjour," "au revoir," "Jé vo aimé,"* and *"Moâ pas parler French."* But he makes fun of a young nationalist waitress who showed him the inscription on a dollar bill and said to him, "See how they treat us! English again, you see. What they ought to say is *une piasse"—piasse* being the corruption of *piastre*, which is colloquially used in French Canada for "dollar." (M. Michel Sanouillet, the author of another nationalist but non-separatist pamphlet, *Le Séparatisme Québecois et Nous*, asserts that in English schools the study of French is still surrounded with "an aura of total uselessness which has made of it the 'sissy subject' that awkward girls and effeminate boys shamefacedly sandwich in between choir practice and home economics." He admits that in Ontario today the situation has somewhat changed and that one occasionally finds Anglophones who speak French so well that they embarrass less cultivated French Canadians. For such Anglophones, he says, the French language has, quite properly, "the rank of *une langue 'noble,'*" which is not usually the case in French Canada.) M. Harvey goes on to enumerate the concessions that have been made to the nationalists—bilingual checks, translation in Parliament and the like—which Marcel Chaput has dismissed as insignificant sops. (To these have been more recently added a royal bilingual and bicultural commission, with André Laurendeau of *Le Devoir* as co-chairman with Davidson Dunton, former chairman of the board of governors of the Canadian Broadcasting Corporation, and a stepping-up of French in the schools in six out of the ten provinces. Premier Jean Lesage has now announced that, by withdrawing from certain federal programs such as hospital insurance, old-age assistance, unemployment insurance and the professional-education plan, the government of Quebec, by 1966, should be getting back forty-seven per cent of all the personal taxes collected.)

In answering M. Chaput, M. Harvey reminds him that the populations of all countries are in the present or have been in the past more or less mixed and that in many several languages are spoken; that if the French minority of the Province of Quebec is going to secede from Canada, why shouldn't the English minority of Westmount or the minority of two or three hundred thousand Jews secede from Montreal [I am told that this estimate is much too high]; that the province, as a matter of fact, may be said to be virtually unilingual already, since at least sixty-five per cent of its population do not know a word of English. And why talk about French Canadian and English Canadian nationality when both groups are more North American than anything else? Nationalism in itself is dangerous. We have seen in Russia and in Germany how the nationalism of either Left or Right quickly turns into the poison of power, and in the nationalism of French Canada it is possible to detect already a tendency to claim for itself a divinely appointed authority. He quotes from a separatist pamphlet: "God did not allot us so many talents without indicating to us that we have a mission to fulfill. . . . We should be proud to serve God in the [human] race. . . . We have become the first missionary people in the whole world." Did the English, whose imperialism has been so denounced in French Canada, express themselves very much differently when they were talking about "the white man's burden"? M. Harvey approves the apothegm of an anonymous Quebec journalist—anonymous on account of this writer's fear of its effect on the separatists—"Nationalism is the imperialism of the poor." And at the present time the French Canadians, far from being one of the most downtrodden minorities, are one of the freest ethnic groups in the world, and though one must of course be vigilant to maintain one's own autonomy "against the tendencies toward centralization," one ought, on the whole, to be glad enough to have the benefit of "British institutions and of the democratic atmosphere of the North American continent. . . . As for me, if I had to choose between national independence with no personal liberty and dependence on a foreign country which would allow me to have that liberty, I should not hesitate to choose the latter."

As for the two billion dollars that French Canada pays to Ottawa in taxes, M. Harvey asserts that Quebec gets most of it back in the federal services, whereas an independent Quebec would have to spend almost two billion in installing army and air and marine forces, in supporting a diplomatic corps, in maintaining its ports and its post office and in paying for public improvements. As for its industry's being owned by foreign capital, that, in the circumstances, was unavoidable. French Canada until not so long ago had not caught up with the industrial revolution. "We lacked everything: education, competence, technique, science, a love of risk, the spirit of sacrifice and the passion for work. Salvation could come to us only from an outside source. It did, and we owe an eternal debt to those who invited it in." Most of the million people who emigrated to the United States went for the work that they could not find in Canada, and we should be grateful to those "chiefs" (such as Duplessis?) who diminished this emigration by "putting a considerable proportion of our forests, our mineral resources and our water power in stronger and more expert hands than our own." But all this gratitude is no longer in order. "Certain privileges that had once to be granted under the pressing necessities of another period should perhaps now be modified or abolished." In regard to French Canadian competence of an administrative and technical kind, M. Harvey is in full agreement with M. Chaput. In the defunct Montreal Light, Heat & Power Company, "hardly any French Canadian occupied a position of real importance. The impression was created that our people were afflicted with a congenital incapacity and that an Anglo-Canadian management or something of the kind was absolutely indispensable. To such a degree that we had begun to believe it ourselves. Then came state ownership with the creation of the Hydro-Quebec. It was possible, by some miracle or other, to reorganize the personnel, to redistribute the work and to assign the responsibilities, and all this was accomplished with ability the major part of which was French Canadian. Did this result in a catastrophe? On the contrary, our engineers, our technicians, our specialists in electronics and the rest performed their tasks so well that nobody would dream of replacing them." We are certainly competent now to take over and run our own industries, but in the meantime let us beware of the separatists when they put at the head of their program "nationalization of the key industries." What exactly do they mean by this? Certain industries should certainly be nationalized, but let us not destroy all personal initiative and freedom of enterprise.

It seems to me significant that that remarkable novelist M. André Langevin, in one of his editorial articles in the French edition of *Maclean's*, should approach the situation in French Canada from an angle prosaically different from that of such separatists as Marcel Chaput. M. Langevin believes that the real "quiet revolution" is that of the Quebec bourgeoisie. When French merchants and bankers went back to France after the English taking-over of French Canada, they left the

"HOW DO YOU SPELL ANN LANDERS?"

Duncan Macpherson. Ann Landers runs a syndicated column of advice to teenagers and married people with problems. *Courtesy of the Toronto* Daily Star

French, as has already been said, with nobody to manage their business, and the British commercial class moved in and built up Quebec trade and banking. But now, says M. Langevin, a French Quebec bourgeoisie has come into existence, in its modern "complex form of executives and technicians," and it will no longer accept English domination.

In its issue of February 8, 1964, *Maclean's* published a kind of joint inquiry by Peter C. Newman and Ralph Allen, who attempted to throw some light on, respectively, the possible line of action to be taken in the crisis with French Canada and the probable results of Quebec's secession. Mr. Newman came to the conclusion that there were only three courses open: to let Quebec go (there is now, it seems, a certain amount of hostile feeling on the part of English Canada); "to form a latter-day Austro-Hungarian Empire by allowing Quebec and the rest of Canada to split into two virtually independent states"; or to reform the Constitution so as to meet the more moderate demands of the French. Mr. Allen, in his attempt to predict what would happen if Quebec seceded, found himself, he says, "in a domain as full of doubt and mystery as Cartier's Gaspé, the sweeping plains of Henry Kelsey and Mackenzie's brooding Rockies." He talked to people all over Canada and elicited the most diverse opinions. Some thought that the withdrawal of this province would drive the others to a closer unity. Others believed that the secession of Quebec would precipitate a general breakup or a collapse of the rest of Canada.

It had been only with difficulty that the Maritime Provinces had, in 1867, been induced to join the Confederation, and New Brunswick and Nova Scotia still identified themselves with New England rather than with Upper Canada, so, following the withdrawal of Quebec, they might well want to attach themselves to the United States. Or they might form a state of their own. A Member of Parliament from the Yukon declared that "the eighteen thousand Canadians who live in the Yukon feel very close to the quarter of a million Americans who live right next door in Alaska. It's a fairly common joke at home that we ought to start a war with Alaska and lose it, so we could become eligible for U.S. foreign aid. It's pretty safe to predict that if Quebec pulls out, there'll be a strong move in the Yukon to do the same." Bruce Hutchison, a well-known journalist and the author of *The Unknown Country* (Canada), believes that Quebec would begin with a Left Wing revolution, then go very far to the Right, become more obscurantist that it already is, be landed in an economic mess and, since the Canadian Confederation would no longer, after its withdrawal, exist, be obliged to seek a union with the United States. It should be noted that twenty-nine per cent of the Canadians, including thirty-three per cent of the inhabitants of Quebec, are reported, again by *Maclean's*, to be in favor of having Canada annexed to the United States, which to us in the United States would seem to be extremely impractical. Would the provinces all become states, or what? Isn't the United States, with

MAN ON THE STREET

Duncan Macpherson. *Courtesy of the Toronto* Daily Star

its adjuncts of Alaska and Hawaii, hard enough to handle already?

Mr. Allen concludes his article with a semi-humorous fantasy of a Balkanized Canada, which he imagines falling back, after forty years, on a conference to discuss "the possibility of uniting the northern half of North America in a single federal nation." The same issue contains a most amusing map, by the cartoonist Lewis Parker, of this fragmented "Nova Balkania." All the little Canadian countries are simultaneously holding World's Fairs. In Westmount, a tiny enclave, a gentleman in a British deerstalker is using a megaphone to broadcast "God Save the Queen" from a flagstaff flying the Union Jack; in the Protectorate of St. Boniface, a de Gaulle-type general in uniform is announcing, to what was once Ontario, *"Nous n'avons aucune ambition territoriale!"*; on an island in Hudson Bay, an Eskimo is shouting "Speak English" to an Eskimo on the mainland of La République de Québec, who threatens him with a revolver and snarls, *"Traître!"* The point of this is that the Quebec nationalists have lately been making a play for the Eskimos who inhabit the upper part of the province and who are dependent on the federal government. A recent expedition to convert them was forced to return on account of the cold and so achieved no results. The Eskimos, it seems, up to now, have referred to the French as "the *oui-oui* people" and regarded them as a kind of demons.

———

THE TERRORISTS. During the night of March 7-8, 1963, three Molotov cocktails—that is, bottles filled with furnace oil—were thrown through the windows of three Montreal armories. The next day, a leaflet was circulated which announced, with much declamation in capitals, a campaign of sabotage:

REVOLUTION BY THE PEOPLE FOR THE PEOPLE
ANNOUNCEMENT TO THE POPULATION OF THE
STATE OF QUEBEC

The QUEBEC LIBERATION FRONT (F.L.Q.) is a REVOLUTIONARY MOVEMENT made up of volunteers who are ready to die for the POLITICAL AND ECONOMIC INDEPENDENCE OF QUEBEC.

The SUICIDE-COMMANDOS of the QUEBEC LIBERATION FRONT (F.L.Q.) have as their principal mission to DESTROY COMPLETELY, by SYSTEMATIC SABOTAGE

a. all colonial (federal) symbols and institutions, especially the R.C.M.P. [Royal Canadian Mounted Police] and the ARMED FORCES,

b. all the media of information in the colonial (English) language which hold us in contempt,

c. all the commercial enterprises and establishments which practice discrimination against the Québecois, which do not use French as their principal language and which put out signs in the colonial language (English),

d. all the factories which discriminate against French-speaking workers.

THE QUEBEC LIBERATION FRONT will proceed to the progressive elimination of all persons collaborating with the powers of occupation.

THE QUEBEC LIBERATION FRONT will also attack all com-

mercial and cultural interests of American colonialism, the
natural ally of English colonialism.

All the volunteers of the F.L.Q. have in their possession
at the moment of committing their actions of sabotage
papers of identification from the REPUBLIC OF QUEBEC. We
demand that our wounded and our prisoners be treated
according to the statute provided for POLITICAL PRISONERS
and according to the GENEVA CONVENTION, in accordance
with the laws of war.

INDEPENDENCE OR DEATH

THE DIGNITY OF THE PEOPLE OF QUEBEC DEMANDS INDE-
PENDENCE.

THE INDEPENDENCE OF QUEBEC IS ONLY POSSIBLE THROUGH
SOCIAL REVOLUTION.

SOCIAL REVOLUTION MEANS A "FREE QUEBEC."

STUDENTS, WORKERS, PEASANTS FORM YOUR SECRET
GROUPS AGAINST ANGLO-AMERICAN COLONIALISM.

The campaign of terror went on for four months.
No arrests were made until June, when sixteen men
were held on suspicion of having been involved in
planting a bomb that had killed a night watchman at
the Recruiting Center of the Canadian Army. These
turned out to be not hoodlums or professional revo-
lutionists but young students, between eighteen and
twenty-five, some of whom came from old and respectable French families. The movement had been
provoked by impatience and disillusion with the apparent inability of the nationalist groups to accomplish anything definite. For these young men, the
idea of seeking reforms through parliamentary methods was not to be taken seriously, and, as Leslie

Roberts has said, the separatists such as Marcel Chaput were "simply talkative old fuddy-duddies." Chaput, with his hunger strikes, news of which had been broadcast on the radio, together with a public statement that his favorite figure in history was Joan of Arc, had made himself a little ridiculous. The time, they believed, had come to strike with something more effective than pamphlets and speeches.

The only inside account, so far as I know, that exists of the F.L.Q. is a book by M. Claude Savoie, *La Véritable Histoire du F.L.Q.* M. Savoie is a Montreal journalist in his early twenties who writes on literature and the arts in the French Canadian press. He had some acquaintance with the terrorists, having been to college with three of them, but he did not belong to their group. He found, however, that he had been included in the list of those who were wanted by the police, and when he presented himself at police headquarters with the object of clearing himself he was locked up for a time with the accused, which afforded him an opportunity to learn a good deal about them. During a midnight conversation in a neighboring cell, he heard a prisoner who was not a terrorist talking to one of the terrorists: "Even supposing that independence is the only solution, I don't see why you have to plant bombs to get it." "Because we don't merely want independence from the national point of view! Chaput can give us that, and it won't change our problem at all! Instead of being exploited by the English in English, we'll be exploited by other English in French. What Quebec needs is a social revolution. The Quebec worker

230

has the same right as anybody else in the world to be sure of steady employment and to be able to have his children educated. A government that was just couldn't tax the income of the father of a family who makes three thousand dollars a year at the same time that it hardly taxes the profits of a big company at all." The F.L.Q., in one of its manifestoes, had denied that it included in its group any member of the Communist Party or of the French O.A.S., and there is, so far as I know, no reason to doubt this, but the language of its literature has evidently been influenced by the former, as its methods seem to have been by the latter.

The group, says M. Savoie, included among its students some professional men and some "bohemians." The chief organizer he describes as "an individual of strange appearance, but about whom one changed one's opinion when one came to know him a little better," and whom he always thereafter refers to as "*l'individu étrange*." The first tiny nucleus was known as the R.R. (Réseau de Résistance), which believed that it was acting in the patriotic tradition of Papineau and Riel. M. Savoie begins with a description of the induction of two of the terrorists. The incident that had the effect of making one of these boys decide to join is typical of the situation in French Canada. Mr. Donald Gordon, the president of the federally owned Canadian National Railways, had, in November, 1962, appeared before a committee of the House of Commons to present a report on his enterprise. He was questioned by French Canadian members as to why out of the twenty-eight top directors none was a French Canadian.

Mr. Gordon denied that this was true. A Lévesque and a Charbonneau were named, and it was pointed out that some French Canadians had such non-French names as O'Hurley. A French member parried this by pointing out that the phrase "Board of Directors" itself implied discrimination; the French of this would be "*direction*." Mr. Gordon explained that he never thought at all about the origins of his associates. He knew that several could speak French. Promotion was based on merit. "The man who, by reason of experience, knowledge, judgment, education or for any other reason, is considered by the management to be the best person for a job will receive the promotion, and we do not care whether he is black, white, red or French." The French member passed on to another grievance: the trainmen do not speak French and cannot be understood by the French passengers. (I am reliably informed by a former employee of the Canadian National Railways that in Ontario, Quebec and the Maritime Provinces all the trainmen have to be bilingual.) Mr. Gordon, under further questioning, insisted that a man's being or not being French had nothing to do with promotion. "You mean to say"—another French member pounced on him—"that in your own judgment there are no French-speaking Canadians with the proper qualities and the capacity to become officers of the company?" "Both of you are distorting what I have said. I am saying that we are not discriminating in connection with our promotions." He seems later to have become a little heated: "Let me say this. . . . As far as I am personally concerned and as long as I am president of the C.N.R., there is not going to be a promotion or an appointment made just because a man is a French Canadian. He has got to be a French Canadian plus other things, and he has to be as able as the other fellow who has a claim on the job. There is going to be fair practice on the C.N.R. as long as I am there. What you are arguing for is discrimination." The distortion that began in the Commons committee was carried further by the fanaticism outside. (The minutes of this hearing have been printed as an appendix to Hugh Bingham Myers' book *The Quebec Revolution* and make it possible to contrast what was really said with the falsified stories that were circulated.) Mr. Gordon, in a newspaper interview, complained that he had been made to say that he would never employ any more French Canadians. French Canada lashed itself into a fury. Demonstrations were held in the streets, at which Gordon was sometimes burned in effigy. The young French Canadian mentioned above, who had not previously hated the English, was present at one of these demonstrations and saw a car belonging to the CKGM radio station driven headlong into the crowd, at the risk of killing people. He thereupon caught the contagion, and, hearing that there was a terrorist group who had planted a bomb in the CKGM station, he decided that he ought to belong to it. Mr. Gordon was to prove his good faith by seriously looking into the matter of the promotion of French Canadians in the C.N.R., and during 1963 many new promotions were made. A new program of recruiting college graduates and students resulted in doubling the number of young French Canadians employed; a French and English education program was instituted; and more bilingual signs, posters and menus are being printed for the passengers of the C.N.R.

But the terrorist movement went on, and its activities became more and more audacious. These young men tried at first to be scrupulous about not allowing anyone to be injured. The three Molotov cocktails that had been thrown into the armories were intended to frighten people but not to set fire or explode. They made very little impression, and it was felt that something more drastic was needed. Some sticks of dynamite were stolen from a subway construction by an innocent-looking ten-year-old boy, whose indignation had been roused by his schoolteacher when she talked to her class of the crimes committed against their ancestors by the English; but before setting these off, the terrorists made a point of warning the management to evacuate the buildings in which the dynamite had been placed. Their compatriots who worked for the "enemy" were stigmatized as "collaborators" and called upon to resign from their jobs. On the twenty-ninth of March, 1963, the statue of General Wolfe was pulled down on the Heights of Abraham, the site of the decisive battle in which the English had beaten the French; the next day, the English retorted by an attack on the Champlain statue in Ottawa. The night of the first of April, a bomb was thrown into the airshaft of the offices of the National Revenue, and the track was broken up on the railroad by which Prime Minister Diefenbaker was travelling from Quebec to Trois-Rivières. The damage was repaired in time, but Diefenbaker was then held up by the announcement that a bomb had been put on the train. Many such false alarms were sent out, but then a really serious accident occurred. Two of the terrorist group in Montreal set out with a bomb to blow up the statue of Sir John Macdonald, the much revered—by the English—Prime Minister who had established the Confederation, but they decided that there were too many people around: somebody might get hurt. They proceeded to Sherbrooke Street, the smartest and most impressive in Montreal, where they discovered a tempting federal building, the Recruiting Center of the Canadian Army. They put a bomb in a garbage pail behind it. When it exploded, it killed a night watchman of whose presence there they did not know. After this, some of the terrorists wanted to quit, but they were reminded that in 1837 the English had not hesitated to string up twenty patriots while the band played *God Save the King*. These youths now conceived the naïve idea that they could correct the bad impression which the killing of the watchman had created by blowing up the headquarters of the Solbec Copper Mines, whose workers had been on strike for months—an exploit which would win them, they imagined, the sympathy of the public. They deposited a bomb in the lavatory, then warned the people in the building. The police were called in, and the bomb was removed.

The next objective was Westmount, the wealthy and attractive residential stronghold of the English population of Montreal. Ten small bombs were deposited in mailboxes. The Westmounters were Anglophone oppressors, and the mailboxes were federal symbols. The bombs were supposed to go off at three o'clock on the morning of May 17th, but not all of them did. One of them exploded in the hands of a sergeant major of the Army who was trying to take out the fuses. He was badly injured and lost an arm. The next day was the Queen's birthday, and some special demonstration was contemplated. The project was to blow up a bridge over the Ottawa River that connects Ottawa with Hull. The police were now more alert. They halted the F.L.Q. car, which contained seventy-five sticks of dynamite, but they did not take the precaution of searching it. They let the boys return to Montreal, where, *faute de mieux*, they celebrated the occasion by putting a bomb near another armory and blowing up four cars that were parked there.

The Army had been complaining of what it thought was a certain lack of zeal on the part of the local police. Some of the separatists who were not involved are said not to have been adverse to the bombings. The police had actually made one raid, but of the fifteen men arrested only one was a member of the F.L.Q. The others belonged to the R.I.N. and a non-violent Socialist group. This put the police in an unfavorable light, and the nationalist organizations protested. After the exploit of the Westmount mailboxes, the Quebec Premier, Jean Lesage, offered a reward of fifty thousand dollars for information that would lead to the arrest of the terrorists. The F.L.Q., on its side, now found that it needed to reorganize. It had been rather

236

undisciplined before. The policy had always been, as is usual in groups that engage in criminal acts, to make sure that every member was compromised by being seriously involved in the bombings, but it was possible for members to take action on their own without notifying what Savoie calls "the Executive." Now the movement was put on a professional basis. By some law of acceleration that seems to operate in such conspiracies, they had been feeling, since the death of the watchman, that, having got themselves so far committed, they had to operate on a larger scale. They could not go on as mere guerrillas. The Executive was henceforth to consist of from five to seven members, with a "national consultative council." Special duties were assigned to the various members: information, arms, medical services, finance, a revolutionary tribunal. The "suicide commandos" were organized in sealed cells of three men each, of whom only one communicated by messenger with a section chief. The head of the cell knew no one but the two other members of his cell, and he did not even know the messengers through whom he received his orders; the two other members knew nobody except the head of the cell. If any of these men was caught, he could not betray the rest of the group, and the only way for the police to get at them was to catch them committing a crime. Yet this complicated scheme did not work. One of their own members, apparently, gave them away. The next five objectives had been settled, and the unit that was appointed for the first of these had, on the evening of June 1st, set out in a car on its mission when it was stopped and arrested by policemen ingeniously disguised as beatniks. Sixteen persons were eventually rounded up, and an inquiry was held at the end of June. While this inquiry was going on, a statue of Queen Victoria in Quebec City was bombed off its pedestal, and its head was found fifty feet away. It was indicated that a monument to the Boer War had also been chosen for destruction. A certain amount of sympathy was manifested for the young rebels, and in *Le Devoir* André Laurendeau protested against the way in which the "preliminary inquiry" was being conducted. Since this was supposed to be a coroner's inquest on the killing of the watchman, the prisoners were not allowed legal defense, and all sixteen—including those who had not known about the bomb—were found criminally responsible for his death. The wife of one of the terrorists was bailed out by an English Mr. Spendlove. When she asked, "Why are you doing this for me, *Monsieur?*," he is supposed to have replied, "Because I understand your nationalism, *Madame*." Ten of these young men got sentences of from three to twelve years.

This caused the dissolution of the F.L.Q., but the terrorist elements reorganized under a slightly different name—l'Armée de Libération du Québec. This seems to have been more effective. There followed, in 1964, a succession of bolder exploits: raids on armories, which provided the terrorists with hand grenades, machine guns and rifles. In one of these, last August in Montreal, five men invaded a gun shop, and when the people in the shop put up a struggle, two of them were shot and killed. A passerby called the police. The building was surrounded, and three of the men were captured as they left the building. A fourth was caught only after a gun battle which moved across a parking lot and in which the man was finally wounded. It was reported in the Montreal *Star* that, according to a statement of the police, the four men were members of the R.I.N.; but this was denied by the president of the organization, who says that only one of them was. The R.I.N. is suing the *Star* for printing the police's statement. In the meantime, on account of Queen Elizabeth's visit, proceedings against the arrested men were temporarily left in abeyance.

There have recently been signs of a severe reaction against the activities of the separatists. The principal paper of Quebec, *La Presse*, has been shut down ever since June as the result of an unsettled conflict between the management and the staff. The president of the R.I.N. has been one of the members of this staff, and the management is apparently bent on the suppression of independent reporting and editorial opinion. The journalists have stubbornly refused to sign an agreement which would subject them to such a censorship. They say that they have "been through fifteen years of silence," when they were muzzled by Duplessis, and that, in surrendering, they would set a precedent for a general policy of suppression on the part of the rest of the press and of the Canadian Broadcasting Corporation. The demonstrations over the Queen's visit put up the backs of the authorities and provoked some official snarlings. A new Attorney General, with a reputation for toughness, has, in reporting on the behavior of the Quebec police, whom he exonerated from charges of unnecessary brutality, rather menacingly bawled out the press and the separatists for inciting to seditious riots. There have been raids on the homes of persons known to be opponents of the government or engaged in trade-union journalism, and a tendency to blame all discontent on Communist infiltration. Among the victims of this, there is said to be an apprehensive feeling that the spirit of Duplessis is reviving. (I have been relying above upon articles by David Oancia in the Toronto *Globe & Mail* and by Robert Mackenzie in the Toronto *Star*.)

THE STRUGGLE AGAINST CENTRALIZATION. The more juvenile aspects of the nationalist movement are partly, of course, the result of the same thirst for thrills, lack of purpose and desperate insubordination that are prevalent today among young people from New York to San Francisco, from Moscow to Paris and London. A recent documentary film, made by the N.B.C., which sent interviewers all over the Province of Quebec to talk with students and young farm and factory workers, revealed, according to a story in the Montreal *Star*, a general bewilderment and discouragement together with a considerable ignorance of what in the way of reform had actually been accomplished by the Lesage administration, in whose policies they claimed to be disappointed. Such opinions as the following were elicited: "I think the old parties are out of date," said a girl with dark glasses in a little village. "What we want is something new. Most of us have the impression that something extraordinary is happening in the Province of Quebec, but we don't know what it is." "More and more we don't believe in anything," said a working girl in Montreal. "The boys are beginning to talk about throwing bombs." Said a boy: "People over fifty can't afford to take risks. But we're young—we can afford to toss a few bombs. You do a few months in jail. It isn't all that bad. It isn't all that important." "This is more than just the clash of two generations," another teen-ager observed. "It is the clash of two different epochs." One does not know exactly what he meant, but this is true in the sense that Quebec, as a non-French Canadian said to me, "is trying to enter the twentieth century." As André Langevin has written in the article referred to above, French Canada has developed a bourgeoisie which wants to have an adequate share in the province's highly profitable business and whose interests coincide at this moment with the impulses of frustrated youth.

But behind French resistance to English Canada, as behind English Canadian resistance to absorption by the United States—and French Canada, too, is partly resistant to this—lies an instinct for self-preservation against the proddings and encroachments of centralized power that is stimulating rebellions all over the world. The great centralized power units such as the Soviet Union and the United States are driving the less powerful units—from a diminished great country like France to a tiny minority like our Iroquois Indians —into extreme nationalistic consciousness. Has there ever been a period in history when the nationalism of minorities manifested itself so intensely? The Hungarians and the lesser Slavic and Balkan peoples are recalcitrant toward the Soviet Union; the states of the old Confederacy are recalcitrant toward our federal government. Our natural moral prejudices in favor of civil rights ought not to conceal from us that the Southerners consider themselves just as much a minority resisting suppression by superior force as the Negroes in resisting them. (One is reminded, in reading the literature of French Canadian separatism, of the constitutional issues raised by the South at the time of the Civil War. Was it or was it not committed to allegiance to the Union?) One sees even minorities in Europe that one had imagined to have settled down to a *modus vivendi* with their differences, reawaking to nationalist resentments. Just as a French Canadian nationalist will walk out of a Montreal restaurant after giving his order in French, if this order is not understood, so a Flemish inhabitant of Belgium will now boycott any restaurant where the menu is printed only in French. In Scotland, a vehement nationalism is demanding, like Quebec, its own parliament. There are no great royal leaders today, few great parliamentary leaders. If a Kennedy shows promise of leadership, his eminence may provoke assassination. What we have today, instead of leaders, are the ever-expanding bureaucracies of government, formidable in machinery,

242

mediocre in personnel—which Kennedy soon discovered he would have to check. One may doubt the sincerity of Duplessis squaring off at what he called the bureaucracy, the "centralizers" of Ottawa; I have encountered English Canadians who complained about this bureaucracy in a similar way. It may be true, as a French Canadian has said to me, that English Canada with her right hand shakes her fist at the United States and with the other sells out to our exploiters, but there is a real fear on the part of both Canadas of having their countries taken away from them and being themselves reduced to serial numbers by the so often still inaccurate computers of Washington which cannot even be expected to make life more endurable when they work with greater accuracy. So the Pole or the Czech or the Magyar dreads the visit of the Moscow official who will tell him how to step up production.

A very curious example of minority nationalism is to be found in Yugoslavia. One had known of three languages in that part of the world, but lately one has been hearing about a fourth—Macedonian. What is now being called Macedonian had up until recently been a group of dialects, but one discovers that these dialects are being combined to produce a new literary language in the interests of the new Macedonian nationalism. The Macedonians have produced some poetry but have not gone beyond short stories in fiction. The University of Skopje has been the headquarters of this Macedonian culture, but apparently the greatest authority on Macedonian language and literature is Professor Horace G. Lunt of Harvard, who published, in

1952, the first full-length Macedonian grammar that has appeared in any language. The Macedonians seem to be proud that Macedonia shares with Bulgaria the distinction, so rare in the Slavic tongues, of possessing a definite article, and that they have even several forms of this, whereas Bulgarian has only one. They are inclined to be snooty about Belgrade, where the Communist officials have too splendid dwellings, and they talk about those Belgrade bureaucrats just as the less docile Russians talk about party officials and the less docile Americans about Washington. An attractive young Macedonian woman came to see me the year before last. She was preparing herself to teach American literature at Skopje University and was working, needless to say, on a thesis on Scott Fitzgerald, who—on account of his romantic and disorderly life?—seems to be a favorite subject, all over Europe, of the students of American Lit. She was on her way back to Yugoslavia when the Skopje earthquake occurred. I had a tragic letter from her from London. The university had been destroyed; several of her family were killed or missing. But she has since sent me several Macedonian books, including verse and prose anthologies. The language, I find, seems so much similar to the other southern Yugoslav languages that one would hardly think it worthwhile to try to create it as—what it has never been—a literary language. Surely such a small minority literature—there are only eight hundred thousand Macedonians living in this immediate area—is something of a morbid symptom.

Yet I am strongly on the side of the peoples who

block the progress of Robert Moses's bulldozers by lying on the ground in front of them, as the Tuscarora Indians did; who shout *"Parlez blanc!"* to reporters who ask questions in English at French Canadian meetings (to which I am told that the retort is likely to be *"Tombez mort!"*); who throw down the red stars of the Soviet Union from the tops of the official buildings and take a blowtorch to the statue of Stalin, as the Hungarians did in 1956. I have even a certain sympathy with de Gaulle—though he has lately been exercising repressions that remind one of the Communist states —when he is recalcitrant about having Europe controlled by the United States. And all power in its recalcitrance to that still uncoördinated, unblended and indigestible Canada that is obstructing assimilation not only abroad but within itself! The problem we all have to face is the defense of individual identity against the centralized official domination that can so easily become a faceless despotism.